UNIVERSITY LIBRARIES

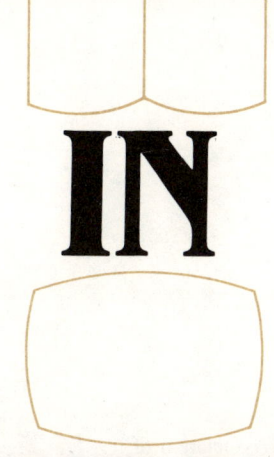

IN

TRANSITION

by
James A. Hyatt
Aurora A. Santiago

NACUBO

© 1987 by the National Association of
   College and University Business Officers
One Dupont Circle
Washington, DC 20036

All rights reserved
Printed in the United States of America
Edited by Lanora Welzenbach

Library of Congress Cataloging-in-Publication Data

Hyatt, James A., 1949–
   University libraries in transition.

   1. Libraries—Automation—Case studies. 2. Library science—Technological innovations. 3. University of Georgia Libraries. 4. Princeton University. Library. 5. University of Illinois (Urbana-Champaign campus). Library. 6. New York University. Libraries. I. Santiago, Aurora A. II. National Association of College and University Business Officers. III. Title.
Z678.9.H9 1986   027.773   86-12819
ISBN 0-915164-29-9

Z
678.9
.H9
1987

FOREWORD

College and university business officers and librarians share a common commitment to the provision of quality service to faculty, students, and other constituencies. Operations of both the business office and the library, however, have been altered dramatically by advances in technology. These changes are apparent in the development of telecommunications systems and the automation of traditional business office and library functions.

In order to promote better understanding of both the scope and the fiscal impact of library automation, NACUBO, with the support of the Council on Library Resources (CLR), conducted a study of library automation at four major research universities. This is a landmark study in that it not only provides a detailed analysis of library automation, but also describes institutional approaches to acquiring and maintaining automated systems.

Business officers, librarians, and others concerned with maintaining academic excellence will benefit from reading this book. A thorough understanding of the scope and economic impact of library automation should result in an informed and responsible approach to institutional decision making.

Pete Reid
President

ACKNOWLEDGMENTS

This book was developed under a grant from the Council on Library Resources (CLR) with guidance from members of the project task force, who were:

Ray Hunt
Vice President for Business and Finance
University of Virginia

William Kirwan
Vice Chancellor for Academic Affairs
University of Maryland

Deanna Marcum
Vice President
Council on Library Resources

Matthew McNulty
Chancellor of Medical Center
Georgetown University

Burton Sonenstein
Vice President for Administration
Wellesley College

Duane Webster
Associate Executive Director
Association of Research Libraries

Martin Cummings and Mark Cain of CLR assisted project staff in the site-visit phase of the project and provided valuable guidance in preparing the text. Paul Kantor of Tantulus, Inc., served as consultant, and project staff also benefited from comments and suggestions of participants of the CLR economic seminars (1983-85). James Brinkerhoff of the University of Michigan was an invaluable source for reference materials.

Case studies were based on site visits and on documents provided by two independent and two public institutions. NACUBO especially appreciates the cooperation of the following resource persons:

Princeton University

Raymond Clark
Comptroller and Associate Treasurer

Donald Koepp
University Librarian

University of Illinois

Craig Bazzani
Vice President for Business and Finance

Hugh Atkinson
University Librarian

Acknowledgments

University of Georgia

Allan Barber
Vice President for Business and
  Finance

David Bishop
Director of Libraries

New York University

Richard Bing
Deputy Vice President for
  Budget and Planning

Anthony Marchionni
Treasurer

Carlton Rochell
Dean, New York University
  Libraries

CONTENTS

FOREWORD iii

ACKNOWLEDGMENTS v

OVERVIEW OF STUDY FINDINGS 1

PRINCETON UNIVERSITY 19

UNIVERSITY OF ILLINOIS 47

NEW YORK UNIVERSITY 67

UNIVERSITY OF GEORGIA 95

OVERVIEW OF STUDY FINDINGS

BACKGROUND

College and university libraries currently are experiencing change both in the ways they provide services and in their responses to rising costs and reduced financial support. These conditions result from three major phenomena: (1) the information explosion, (2) the technology revolution, and (3) escalating library costs.

The Information Explosion. According to a report issued by the Association of Research Libraries and the Research Libraries Group, Inc., the amount of published material is increasing rapidly, at about 2.5 percent each year, and libraries are losing ground in the proportion of new information they are able to purchase.[1] In addition, Seibert, Rider, and others indicate that the size of research library collections tend to double every 16 to 20 years. In Seibert's study of nine "older" research libraries, the size of an average collection grew from 1.29 million volumes in 1938 to 4.15 million volumes by 1980.[2]

In addition to being available in print, information is found in a variety of other formats, ranging from audio cassettes to video discs. Thus, there is increasing demand for library services at a time when libraries are experiencing economic pressure to reduce or contain operating costs.

The Technological Revolution. The manner in which libraries catalog, store, and retrieve information has changed dramatically in recent years. These changes result from at least five important developments in library automation. First, development of the Machine-Readable Cataloging or MARC system by the Library of Congress enabled libraries to create machine-readable bibliographic files. Second, establishment of computer library networks, such as the Ohio College Library Center (OCLC) and the Research Libraries Information Network (RLIN) permitted libraries to use machine-readable cataloging done by other libraries, as well as to submit their own cataloging to the networks. Third, automation of certain key library functions, such as cataloging and bibliographic control, interlibrary loans, acquisitions, and circulation, has changed organizational structures and staffing patterns at many leading academic and public libraries. Fourth, development of online public access catalogs, or OPACs, enabled library users to obtain bibliographic information without resorting to time-consuming, manual card catalogs.

Finally, creation of local area computer networks or LANs permitted library users to access library information without having to be physically present in the library. These developments, combined with growing information resources, provided library users with access to more information and enabled them to make more effective use of library resources. Such changes, however, also required an increasing investment of institutional resources in library operations.

Escalating Library Costs. While library collections expanded, library costs were rising. In the last decade, U.S. periodical prices quadrupled and hardcover book prices tripled. According to a report issued by the Association of Research Libraries and the Research Libraries Group, Inc.,

> The costs of running research libraries are increasing faster than university budgets can accommodate. Association of Research Libraries statistics indicate the magnitude of the cost increases for both library materials and personnel—the two major costs in research libraries. From 1968-69 to 1978-79, ARL member libraries spent 91% more for library materials, yet added 22.5% fewer books to their collections. Personnel costs have increased 106% in the same period, yet essentially no new positions have been added. When such data are corrected for inflation, the magnitude of the problem doubles.[3]

In addition to rising costs, colleges and universities also have contended with diminishing levels of federal, state, and local support, thus attempting to maintain academic excellence in a climate of economic austerity.

Objectives of NACUBO Study

To assist colleges and universities in meeting the challenges outlined above, the National Association of College and University Business Officers (NACUBO), under a grant from the Council on Library Resources (CLR), conducted a study of ways in which four universities and their libraries have responded to technological change. The primary objectives of the study were:
1. To examine the management and planning of university libraries within the context of overall institutional goals and objectives.
2. To examine the impact of technological changes on library operations, with regard to both current and future activities.

Institutions participating in the study represented both public and independent sectors of higher education and were located in both rural and urban areas. This insured that study results would be useful to a broad range of institutions. In addition, institutions selected had to have demonstrated leadership in both library management and use of technology to enhance library operations. Consideration also was given to institutions that had developed their own automated systems or who had adapted external systems.

Institutions that agreed to participate in the study were: (1) Princeton University, (2) the University of Illinois at Urbana-Champaign, and (3) New York University, and (4) University of Georgia. Their experiences in responding to technological change formed the basis for the case studies presented here.

When reviewing this material, it is important to recognize that management processes and automated systems of these organizations were developed within unique sets of environmental factors. One should be cautious in comparing automated systems or management processes of any one institution to others in the study. Rather, the benefit of these case studies lies in noting how each institution and its library responded to technological change within the context of its institutional goals, objectives, and priorities.

PROJECT DESIGN AND METHODOLOGY

The project consisted of three principal phases. First was the collection and analysis of background information for the institution and its library, including financial statements and budgets and plans for the institution, the library, and automated systems.

The project's second phase involved site visits to the four institutions, during which NACUBO staff interviewed key campus administrators, including the president or chief executive officer, chief academic officer, chief financial officer, director of libraries, director of the computer center, and others. Major issues addressed during site visits were: the library's role in institutional planning, budgeting, and other management processes; networking, particularly the use of bibliographic utilities; membership in consortia such as the Research Libraries Group (RLG); and library plans for initiating and responding to changing funding levels, user needs, and institutional priorities.

The third phase of the study involved documentation of site visit findings as case studies and preparation of an overview paper that highlighted the study results.

DESCRIPTIONS OF LIBRARY STUDIED

Each case study includes detailed profiles for both the institution and its library. Exhibits I, II, and III in this chapter diagram institutional

EXHIBIT I

Institutional Characteristics of Study Participants
(Approximate % for 1983-84)

	University of Georgia	Princeton University	University of Illinois	New York University
Control	Public	Independent	Public	Independent
FTE Enrollment[1]	23,847	6,200	34,830	23,267
Primary Sources of Education & General Support[2]	State (55%)	Student Fees (31%) Investment Income (24%)	State (42%)	Student Tuition and Fees (70%)

Source: 1. ARL Statistics, 1983-84
2. Institutional fact books from site visit institutions

EXHIBIT II

Library Characteristics of Study Participants

	University of Georgia	Princeton University	University of Illinois	New York University
Branch Libraries	7	25	39	7
STAFF				
Professional	74	97	120	97
Nonprofessional	163	227	295	178
Student	87	58	128	68
Total	324	382	543	343
Volumes Held	2,316,499	3,636,334	6,615,550	2,815,357

Source: ARL Statistics, 1983-84

and library characteristics. When reviewing these exhibits, note that Princeton University and New York University are heavily dependent on tuition, fees, and private support. Seeking and maintaining sufficient external support through fund-raising activities are, therefore, critical to the operations of these institutions and of their libraries. Also important are differences in the percentage of the university's total educational and general expenditures attributable to its library. Princeton

Overview

EXHIBIT III

Library Expenditures (ARL Questionnaire, 1983-84)
(All figures in thousands)

	University of Georgia	Princeton University	University of Illinois	New York University
Salary (exclude fringe)	$3,546 (48.2%)	$6,354 (56.1%)	$7,454 (54.8%)	$5,704 (56.8%)
Materials	3,095 (42.1%)	3,297 (29.1%)	4,369 (32.2%)	3,060 (30.5%)
Other Operating Expenses (including binding)	714 (9.7%)	1,683 (14.8%)	1,763 (13.0%)	1,271 (12.7%)
Total	$7,355 (100%)	$11,334 (100%)	$13,586 (100%)	$10,035 (100%)
Percent of Total Education & General	2.6%	7.5%	3.4%	2.5%

University library accounts for approximately 7 percent of institutional educational and general expenditures. For the libraries of New York University and the University of Georgia, this percentage is closer to 2.5.

These percentages do not connote relative importance placed on the library by its respective institution; rather, they reflect the different missions, organizational structures, operational processes, and priorities of each institution and its library. Differences in environment and mission, which are highlighted in the case studies, have done much to shape institutional approaches to library automation.

RESPONDING TO TECHNOLOGICAL CHANGE

A Framework for Analysis

An institution's ability to capitalize on new opportunities frequently depends on its administrators' ability to ask the right questions. In deciding how to approach library automation, the following questions are useful.

1. Do business officers and librarians understand the impact of the information and technological revolutions on library operations?

2. Do they understand the costs associated with library automation?
3. Do current planning practices of libraries and institutions take into consideration the effect of the information and technological revolutions and the rising costs of library operations?
4. Are libraries organized such that they can capitalize on the technological revolution? Are they involved in institutional allocation decisions?
5. Are libraries in a position to effect change, that is, is the message getting through to institutional decision makers?
6. What is the state of the art in library automation at the institutions visited?
7. How will library automation benefit the user?
8. Will automation reduce operating costs?
9. How will library automation be paid for?
10. Are the benefits of automation quantifiable and is cost-benefit analysis possible?

The following responses are based on (1) experiences of institutions visited for this study; (2) a review of the literature; and (3) discussions with librarians and business officers who participated in three seminars on the Economics of Research Libraries (1983-85), which were sponsored by the Council on Library Resources (CLR).

Awareness of Technology. At the institutions visited, the impact of the information and technological revolutions appeared to be well understood by senior library administrators and generally understood by senior university administrators. The understanding of senior university administrators depended on how effective the university librarian had been in educating them concerning library automation. For example, senior administrators appeared to be aware of the capabilities of the online public access catalog (OPAC), but a smaller number of both institutional administrators and librarians understood the connection between OPAC and the institution's local area computer network (LAN) or the mechanism by which institutionwide access to OPAC would be provided.

Awareness of Cost. In general, there is an inadequate understanding on the part of both librarians and senior administrators of the costs of library automation. With regard to the online public access catalog, which many librarians believe to be the cornerstone of library automation, Lawrence, Matthews, and Miller note that:

> Despite the importance of the topic, no one really knows how much it costs to provide an online catalog. Certainly estimates are available, and contract figures and purchase costs for various systems are announced almost daily. However, few, if any, library administrators know how much it costs to acquire and operate their online catalog,

or how much money is saved (if any) by its implementation. This may be because libraries are reluctant to talk about their cost experience, or because the online catalog touches so many aspects of library operations that it is impossible to separate out the costs attributable solely to the online catalog (OLC).[4]

Attempts have been made, however, to estimate total costs of library automation. According to an Association of Research Libraries member survey, of whom 62 responded, aggregate one-time expenditures for startup and upgrades in equipment, and peripheral or external services as of 1984 totaled $25,816,157. Ongoing or annual costs for the 62 respondents were $19,210,806 in continuing contracts, and $8,103,892 in continuing local costs for a total of $27,314,698. This resulted in average annual costs of $440,560 for each respondent.[5]

The Report of the Director of Libraries, University of Pennsylvania, 1982-83, includes an example of the cost of library automation for an individual research institution. A plan for implementing new technology is presented, with cost figures as follows:

1. Development and implementation of a comprehensive computer network and online catalog called PENNLIN $1,500,000
2. Catalog Conversion.. 1,800,000
3. Electronic Access to Resources 500,000
   Total Amount Required................................. $3,800,000[6]

In their study of the costs of online catalogs, Lawrence, Matthews, and Miller concluded that:

- For most academic libraries, basic systems will cost something on the order of $200,000 to acquire and about $20,000 per year to maintain.
- For large academic libraries, basic systems will cost around $500,000 to $600,000 to acquire and about $50,000 per year to maintain.
- Financing automated systems appears to be a greater budgetary burden for smaller academic libraries.*
- Starting from the online catalog as a system base, added system functions increase cost about 10 percent each, both initially and annually.
- The cost of adding various features to the online catalog itself cannot be determined at present, but it appears to be at minimum somewhat less than the cost of adding new functions, but at most

---

*In reviewing the above figures, it should be noted that these amounts are in 1983 dollars and that the cost estimates do not include several important cost categories, notably (a) creating and maintaining the bibliographic database, (b) operating costs for telecommunication lines, and (c) added storage for database expansion over time.

(e.g., keyword searching) may be much greater than the cost of adding functions.[7]

As indicated by the cost figures presented above, library automation is not an inexpensive undertaking. Why, then, is there a lack of good cost data on library automation? First, the full cost of library automation may not be reflected in the library's budget. Certain items, such as computer hardware or software, may be purchased centrally and shown in the budget of the institution as a whole. Second, charges for computer time or for technical personnel provided by a central computer facility may not be reflected in the library's budget. Third, a complete picture of automation costs may not be possible if automated systems are acquired in a gradual or piece-by-piece fashion.

Planning for Library Automation. Formal strategic planning for automation is rare both within the library and at the senior administrative level; instead, such planning is integrated into other institutional activities. At Princeton and New York universities, for example, planning for automation was tied to institutional development or fund-raising efforts. At the University of Georgia, library automation proceeded in an evolutionary fashion with formal planning for automation occurring only during the last few years. Further, at two of the institutions visited, Illinois and New York universities, formal five-year plans only recently have been prepared or are being prepared for all major units.

If library automation is so important, why haven't libraries and institutions engaged in more formal planning? First, the technology has been changing rapidly and the number of automated systems available from vendors has been limited. In a report prepared by the Research Libraries Group, Inc., titled *Processing and Data Distribution within the Research Libraries Information Network*,[8] no local system received unanimous endorsement. Recommended with reservations were the BLIS system from Biblio-Techniques, Inc.; the GEAC system from GEAC Ltd.; and the NOTIS system from Northwestern University. Libraries have tended to acquire systems on a trial basis, for example, Princeton's functional test of the Carlyle online catalog system, or have waited until tested systems were available.

A second reason that libraries have not engaged in formal planning is that once automated systems are acquired, they soon become obsolete. According to Lawrence, Matthews, and Miller,

> Any decision that commits the library for a period longer than about seven years is a wrong decision.[9]

The Library's Role in Allocation Decisions. All library directors at the site-visit universities understood the decision-making and allocation processes at their own institutions. Consequently, they were successful in garnering at least administrative backing for library automation, and in some instances have received specific support for automation. Making a case for library automation, however, is extremely difficult when institutions are under increasing pressure to reduce costs and limit expenditures. Librarians who have been successful in obtaining institutional support have stressed the importance of the library to the advancement of the institution as a whole. Martin, for example, noted that:

> . . . information provision is a significant proportion of the cost of all educational and research programs, and should be recognized as such. A library that is perceived solely as an overhead expenditure is extremely vulnerable to budgetary manipulation.[10]

In terms of managerial flexibility or the ability to reallocate library budgets, all institutions visited provided their director of libraries with some degree of management flexibility. At Princeton University, for example, salary savings were used to partially offset the costs of library automation. Given the escalating costs of library materials, however, internal reallocation of library budget cannot be viewed as a sole source of support for library automation.

On the whole, librarians are not as involved in planning and budgetary decisions as they should be. As a result, they frequently do not understand how budget decisions are made and have little influence over the way resources are allocated. According to Martin, however, this situation may be changing:

> Even the act of financial planning costs money and one may expect to see more library appointments of budget and business officers and planning assistants.[11]

Is the Message Getting Through? Based on experiences of site-visit institutions, the issue of library automation is gaining importance on campus for several reasons. First, today's consumer of library services is more technologically sophisticated than in the past. Students, faculty, and researchers expect instantaneous information at their choice of location and time. Second, growth in local area computer networks or LANs that link library resources to computer terminals or microcomputers throughout the campus will create a demand for greater access to automated library systems, such as OPAC. Third, increasing costs of printed material are causing both librarians and senior administrators to reassess the manner in which information is stored, accessed, and retrieved.

Given these conditions, are libraries in a position to effect change?

University Libraries in Transition

Librarians who wish to maintain a tradition of the library as a collection of printed material and who strive to increase such collections and their material budgets will have little impact. However, librarians who perceive the library as an information center and who seek to provide services at the convenience of their users can enhance the library's role in the academic and research activities of their institutions.

State of the Art in Library Automation. Exhibits IV and V in this chapter provide illustrations of the types of national data bases and the

---

EXHIBIT IV

Use of National Databases

	Georgia	Princeton	Illinois	NYU
National Networks				
OCLC	X		X	
RLIN		X		X
Function				
Cataloging	X	X	X	X
Acquisition (monographs)				X
Interlibrary Loan	X	X	X	X
Collection Development		X		X
Provide Database Searches? (DIALOG, BRS, etc.)	YES	YES	YES	YES

EXHIBIT V

Local Automated Systems

	Georgia	Princeton	Illinois	NYU
Automated Systems				
Primary System	MARVEL	GEAC/Carlyle*	LCS/FBR	GEAC (Bobcat)
Where Developed?	Local	External	Local/External	External (Bobcat Local/Ext.)
Integrated?	Yes	No	No	No
Functions	X	X	X	X
Circulation				
Reserve		X	X	X
Acquisition (Monographs)	X	X	X	
Serials		X	X	
Online Cat.	X*	X*	X	X
III			X	

*Prototypes or demonstrations systems.

Overview

configuration of local automated systems in use at site-visit institutions. Below are listed typical components of an automated library system.

1. Access to one of the national computer networks, either the Ohio College Library Network (OCLC) or the Research Libraries Information Network (RLIN). These networks permit members to obtain machine-readable cataloging done by other libraries, including the Library of Congress, and help to contain the amount of retrospective conversion (the process by which manual records for library materials are converted to machine-readable form) required by individual libraries.
2. Local automated systems that provide the following functions:
   a. cataloging
   b. acquisitions
   c. interlibrary loans
   d. collection development
3. Integration of the libraries' automated systems, such as the online public access catalog, with an institution-wide telecommunications network, comprised of computer terminals and access ports known as a local area network or LAN. According to a study conducted by the Research Library Group, Inc. (RLG), the average research institution LAN will have acquired 800 devices (terminals and workstations) with access to the online catalog by the mid-1980s and will grow to 1,500 devices by the late 1980s.[12]

As noted in Exhibits IV and V, all institutions visited are members either of OCLC or RLG. Only one library, at the University of Georgia, developed its own inhouse automated system (MARVEL). The other three institutions acquired their systems either from commercial vendors, such as GEAC or Carlyle, or from other institutions, such as Ohio State University. According to a survey by Peat, Marwick, Mitchell & Co., there is a growing movement among both academic and public libraries toward acquiring turnkey systems. The survey states:

> The library automation marketplace has undergone tremendous changes. The turnkey systems now available in the marketplace are perceived as greatly improved over earlier systems, in software as well as hardware. This change parallels the growth in sophistication of librarians involved in automation. As a result of improvements in the library automation marketplace, more libraries consider purchasing a turnkey system rather than developing a system inhouse.[13]

All the institutions visited are planning for, or are in the process of installing, local area networks. Only at New York University, however, does the dean of libraries serve on the LAN planning committee. At the other institutions, directors of libraries are aware of the LAN and expect the library system to be an integral part of it. They do not, however, feel a need to be intimately involved in its planning or implementation. Based on the experience of site-visit institutions, an online public access catalog is an essential component of any automated system. According to Lawrence, Matthews, and Miller, there are five ways of acquiring such a system.[14]

1. *Service Bureau.* An external organization provides online catalog services through terminals placed in the library. Examples of library automation service bureaus include OCLC, Inc. and the Research Libraries Information Network. Examples of online catalog service bureaus are Inforonics, Avatar Systems, and the Carlyle Systems.
2. *Turnkey Vendor Approach.* An external organization provides a specialized hardware/software package containing the online catalog. Examples of turnkey systems are CLSI and GEAC.
3. *Local Hardware, Purchased Software.* An institution procures and maintains computer hardware and separately purchases the online catalog software. Examples of purchased software are the University of Illinois system, with software purchased originally from Ohio State University and run on campus computing equipment.
4. *Local Software, Service Bureau Hardware.* An institution is responsible for specification, development, and implementation of its online catalog software, which may include the catalog proper and the database management system. An example of this approach is the Minnesota State University system.*
5. *In-House Approach.* An institution specifies programs and implements the catalog on hardware procured and maintained by the institution. The University of Georgia is an example of this approach. As noted earlier, this university was the only institution visited that developed an online system internally.

User Benefits. Improved service to library users should be a major consideration in the development of automated library systems. Benefits to library users identified at site-visit institutions included:

1. *Improved Access to Library Materials.* By cataloging online all books (for which there is a Library of Congress cataloging copy) at time of receipt, the Princeton library has cut processing time to a minimum. Twenty-five percent of the books received in 1983-84 were cataloged and on the shelf within 48 hours of their arrival in the library. At Illinois University, a statewide library computer

---

*A general estimate of the costs of implementing an online catalog was discussed in a previous section. Cost estimates for each of the approaches outlined above are contained in the Lawrence, Matthews, and Miller study (see References).

system (LCS) provides information about author, title, location, and availability of nearly all the university library's 7 million volumes and of volumes in 25 other academic libraries in Illinois. In addition, user access to materials is made possible through a statewide Interlibrary Delivery System (ILDS). In the case of interlibrary loans, 80 percent of the time a book is placed on a loading dock within 24 hours and mailed to a user within two days.
2. *Improved Reference Capabilities.* With online public access catalogs (OPAC), users can identify whether the library has a specific item and, if so, its location. According to users of Princeton's Carlyle system:

> It provides a quick and painless way of finding research information which might otherwise be overlooked amid the clutter of millions of catalog cards.

Research and practice also indicate that once library patrons have been exposed to OPAC, user demand increases.
3. *Scholars' Workstation.* Through using local area networks (LANs), library users can access the OPAC at their convenience. It is conceivable that in the future a scholar, through the use of a campus LAN, will be able to access information not only from his or her institution's library, but also from national and international library networks. Such access to a "data information highway" would benefit both students and faculty and enhance the quality of research and instructional activities.

Will Automation Reduce Operating Costs? Automation frequently is introduced to achieve either increased efficiency or to enhance effectiveness. Automated library systems, however, do not result in reduced operating costs. According to Mick:

> Computer hardware and software vendors offer the seductive temptations of reduced labor costs and increased production through automation, but although system performance may improve, overall costs rarely go down.[15]

Furthermore, according to Bauman and Blackman, the motivation for automation is often not *financial* but *service-oriented* and is designed to obtain better control over the library collection.[16]

Failure to achieve cost reductions is due in part to the need for hiring more sophisticated personnel to operate automated systems or for upgrading the skills of the existing staff. In this regard Veaner notes that:

> For every decline in (computer) hardware costs, there appears to be a corresponding greater increase in the costs of the staff required to support this hardware.[17]

At Princeton, 38 support staff processing positions (out of 70 audited positions) were reclassified to reflect the need for more sophisticated technical knowledge. Currently all processing staff and most public service librarians at Princeton use either RLIN or one or more of the library's other automated systems, and more than half the staff use both.

How Will Automation Be Paid For? There are four principal sources of support for library automation. First is internal reallocation of existing resources, as with Princeton University, which used salary savings to partially fund automation. Second is the specific allocation of funds from either the central administration, as with the University of Georgia, or through state appropriations, as in the case of the University of Illinois, which received state support to develop its statewide library network. Consortial arrangements with other local libraries form a third source of support, for example, New York University's consortium with the New School for Social Research, Parsons School of Design, and Cooper Union. The fourth source is private gifts or foundation grants, as in the case of New York University.

From the results of site visits, it appears that independent institutions rely heavily on private gifts or foundation and corporate grants to fund automation. Public institutions, while soliciting corporate or foundation support, tend to rely either on allocations from the central administration or specific line items in state appropriations. This pattern is consistent with traditional sources of support for public and independent institutions. However, given continued reductions in state and federal support for higher education, it appears likely that public institutions also will turn more to private donors and foundations to fund library automation.

Is Cost-Benefit Analysis of Automation Possible? Considering the amount of institutional resources required to fund library automation, it appears that some form of cost-benefit analysis of automated systems is not only desirable, but necessary. Thus far, such analysis has been hindered by the absence of comprehensive costs data on automation and by lack of concrete indexes or measures of its benefits. A thorough assessment of costs and benefits of automation had not been conducted at the institutions visited, although administrators at Princeton and New York universities have sought user reaction to the online public access catalog.

CONCLUSION

Based on the experience of site-visit institutions in developing and implementing automated systems, several conclusions can be drawn relative to the following major areas:

1. Extent to which site-visit institutions and their libraries achieved the objectives they established for themselves.
2. Utility of study findings to other librarians and administrators.
3. Future developments in library automation.

Were Institutional and Library Objectives Met? Given the absence of formal planning documents related to automation at the libraries visited, a more appropriate question may be "Are the libraries and institutions satisfied with their automated systems?" It appears that while existing systems still need some refinements, the majority of librarians and administrators interviewed were satisfied with them. Formal planning for automation is important. In this regard, the University of Georgia libraries indicated that they were establishing specific objectives and criteria as a basis for future evaluation of automated systems.

Utility of Study Findings to Other Institutions and Their Libraries. The following study findings are useful to libraries currently involved in automating or planning automated library systems.

1. *Automated library systems do not reduce current operating costs.* Benefits associated with automated systems relate more to improved service than to reduced costs.
2. *Success of automated systems is dependent on careful planning.* In selecting or developing an automated system, adequate time must be provided for input from library users and staff. In addition, care should be taken in developing systems specifications, in selecting an appropriate vendor, and in establishing performance criteria and penalties for vendor noncompliance.
3. *There is a trend toward acquiring turnkey systems.* Due to improvements in technology and the prohibitive costs of developing "homegrown" systems, more and more libraries are using turnkey systems. Both Princeton University and New York University have installed turnkey systems, partly because they desire fully integrated library systems and partly because of recent advances in turnkey capabilities.
4. *There is an increasing emphasis on integrated library systems.* According to a recent study by Mann, Chao, and Hughes, more libraries are planning integrated systems:

> The ability for integrating various library functions plays an important part in choice of hardware and software. The shift towards turnkey systems is a reflection of a trend toward integrated systems. The cost of developing an integrated system by one institution alone is prohibitively high; turnkey system vendors can spread development cost among a number of library clients.[18]

The experiences of New York University and Princeton University tend to support this conclusion.

5. *There is increasing emphasis on distributed versus centralized systems.* Computerized information systems at colleges and universities are evolving from centralized systems with a computer center at their core to distributed systems that place both information and information access closer to the user. Such a system of distributed computing is frequently termed a "library model." In part, institutions are moving toward such an approach because of proliferating computer workstations and the desire of computer users to link these workstations into an intercampus computer network or local area network (LAN). The emphasis at all site-visit institutions was on distributed computing and they were all either planning for or implementing local area networks. Whether such an approach will result in fewer branch libraries is still not known.

6. *Changing relationships between libraries and campus computer centers.* The same technology that stimulated development of automated library systems, especially the online public access catalog, also is affecting operations of campus computer centers. In an article on the possible merger of libraries and computer centers, Neff notes that:

Libraries and computer centers will tend to have the same types of devices for archival storage and it will not matter which organization actually controls the devices, because a union catalog of all institutional information, including data and software, will exist.[19]

It is apparent from the case studies presented here that, rather than competing with one another, libraries and computer centers have been cooperating to better address users' needs. According to the director of libraries at the University of Georgia "one of the biggest problems of library directors relative to automation is that they try to do the computer center's job. They try to make decisions that the computer center should make."

Future of Library Automation. Librarians at site-visit institutions foresee several major improvements and developments in library automation. First, increased access to various local area networks will allow users to search and retrieve information from a wide range of data bases throughout the world. Such access will further the concept of LANs as "data highways." Second, libraries will have to provide provisions for machine-readable, nonbibliographic data. According to Hugh Atkinson of the University of Illinois, "the real challenge for the next two decades will be the rise of economic data, census data, voting records, survey data of all kinds, and a mass of chemical and bibliographic data in machine-readable form." Another major issue, according to Atkinson, involves use of the electronic journal and reference book. In his opinion, such developments will alter radically the manner in which faculty and students use library services.

Finally, all institutions visited predicted the rise of a new role for the library, which would involve use of a distributed information system and would bring library resources to users rather than bringing users to the library. Information provided in this manner will be in a form prescribed by the user and will be available at his or her discretion. Neff notes that:

> The service that will be in great demand when it becomes practical is document delivery from the library to the workstation. This service would include the electronic card catalog and circulation systems as well. The concept is that users search for the book or serial they want and then the computer delivers it page by page to the workstation display.[20]

Summary

In summary, automated systems provide exciting opportunities for the library to better serve university needs. But automation also requires commitment of significant institutional resources. Given these facts, it is incumbent on both librarians and business officers to keep informed of current developments in automation technology and of the relevant experiences of other institutions. The case studies that follow provide a useful reference for those interested in pursuing a proactive and informed approach to library automation.

REFERENCES

1. "The Economic and Financial Management of Research Libraries." A Report in an Exploratory Meeting Sponsored by the Associates of Research Libraries and the Research Libraries Group Inc., Washington, D.C.: October 1981.
2. Seibert, Warren F. "How Libraries Grow: A Brief Look Backward (and Forward)," *Journal of Academic Librarianship*, vol. 11, no. 1 (March 1985), pp. 19-23.
3. Report from Exploratory Meeting of the Association of Research Libraries and Research Libraries Group.
4. Lawrence, Gary S.; Matthews, Joseph R.; and Miller, Charles E. "Costs and Features of Online Catalogs: The State of the Art," *Information Technology and Libraries*, December 1983.

5. *The Automation Inventory of Research Libraries.* Washington, D.C.: Office of Management Studies, Association of Research Libraries, 1985.
6. De Gennaro, Richard. *Into the Information Age: Report of the Director of Libraries, University of Pennsylvania, 1982-83.*
7. *Information Technology and Libraries,* Section 4.4, December 1983.
8. *Processing and Data Distribution within the Research Libraries Information Network.* Stanford, CA: Research Libraries Group Inc. (RLG), 1983.
9. *Information Technology and Libraries,* Section 5.2, December 1983.
10. Martin, Murray S. "Financial Planning: New Needs, New Sources, New Styles," in *Financing Information Services, Problems, Changing Approaches, and New Opportunities for Academic and Research Libraries.* Edited by Peter Spyers-Duran and Thomas W. Mann, Jr. *New Directions in Librarianship,* no. 6, p. 100.
11. Ibid, p. 103.
12. *Processing and Data Distribution within the Research Libraries Information Network,* RLG, Inc.
13. Mann, Thomas W. Jr.; Chao, Yuan Tsien D.; and Hughes, K. Scott. *Library Automation: A Survey of Leading Academic and Public Libraries in the United States,* San Francisco: Peat, Marwick, Mitchell & Co., February 1986, p. 3.
14. *Information Technology and Libraries,* Section 3.2, December 1983.
15. Mick, C.K. "Cost Analysis of Information Systems and Services." *Annual Review of Information Science and Technology,* no. 14, 1979, pp. 37-64.
16. Baumol, William J. and Blackman, Sue Anne Batey. "Electronics, the Cost Disease, and the Operation of Libraries," *Journal of the American Society for Information Science.*
17. Veaner, A.B. "What Hath Technology Wrought?" F.W. Lancaster, ed. *Problems and Failures in Library Automation: Proceedings of the 1978 Clinic on Library Applications of Data Processing.* Urbana-Champaign, IL: University of Illinois Graduate School of Library Sciences, 1979.
18. Peat, Marwick, Mitchell & Co., *Library Automation,* pp. 3-4.
19. Neff, Raymond K. "Merging Libraries and Computer Centers: Manifest Destiny or Manifestly Deranged? An Academic Services Perspective," EDUCOM Bulletin vol. 20/no. 4 (Winter 1985), p. 9.
20. Ibid, p. 11.

PRINCETON UNIVERSITY

"Everyone at Princeton will always have at least one thing in common: the Library."
Donald W. Koepp
University Librarian

BACKGROUND

To understand the management processes of an organization, one must first understand the environment, both internal and external, in which it operates. Described below are organizational profiles for Princeton University and its library.

Institutional Profile

Undergraduate Programs. Princeton's undergraduate programs (A.B. and B.S.E.) are designed to achieve both breadth and depth; each student must satisfy both a set of distribution requirements and requirements in his or her area of concentration. There are 46 departments and programs from which students may select such areas, with undergraduate concentration patterns remaining fairly stable over the years. The ten largest areas of concentration in 1983-84 were:

Department	Number of Concentrators
History	259
Politics	212
English	189
Economics	183
Biology	142
Electrical Engineering and Computer Science	136
Woodrow Wilson School	125
Civil Engineering	108
Psychology	106
Mechanical and Aerospace Engineering	104

Graduate Programs. The graduate school, established in 1900, enrolls approximately 1,500 students in 53 fields and departments. By history and design, the school is relatively small and traditionally has emphasized Ph.D. programs in the arts and sciences. During 1983-84, Princeton awarded 216 Ph.D.s and 361 master's degrees. The enrollment of graduate students by academic division for 1984-85 is approximately:

Division	Number
Humanities	350
Social Sciences	235
Natural Sciences	450
School of Engineering and Applied Science	260

School of Architecture	65
Woodrow Wilson School	140

Faculty. The total number of faculty in 1983-84, including visitors and part-time faculty, was 824. This number included 337 professors, 63 associate professors, 186 assistant professors, 15 instructors, 142 lecturers, and 81 visitors. Sixty-five percent of the professorial faculty is tenured.

Scholarship and Research. Scholarship and research are essential to Princeton's educational purposes. Every faculty member is engaged in scholarly research, and each year Princeton's faculty is responsible for more than 2,000 published scholarly documents. In addition, graduate students and undergraduates are expected to pursue their own independent research projects, a factor that has significant impact on library use and on the size and scope of its collection.

One measure of the university's commitment to research is the extent of externally supported project activity on campus. In 1983-84, external sources provided funding for more than 700 separate projects, excluding those of the Plasma Physics Laboratory. Approximately 330 projects were in natural sciences, 200 were in engineering and applied sciences, and 140 were in humanities and social sciences. Total funding for these projects was $30 million, of which 90 percent came from the government, 5 percent from foundations, and 5 percent from industry and other sources. This level of externally funded research creates a significant demand for library services.

Library Profile

The Princeton University library system consists of the Harvey S. Firestone Memorial Library, which houses the largest portion of Princeton's collection, and 22 special libraries, including 15 academic department collections. There are more than 3.5 million books and 31,000 current periodical subscriptions in the library. Except for rare books, all volumes are in open stacks. In the Firestone Library, stacks are open to the university community but closed to others. Total library expenditures for 1983-84 were approximately $11,300,000; for 1984-85 the budget is estimated at $13,200,000, which includes more than $3,500,000 for acquisitions (*A Princeton Profile 1984-85*).

Total library expenditures represent approximately 7.5 percent of Princeton's total educational and general expenditures. This percentage is high compared to that of other members of the Association of Research Libraries, and is a function of (1) a commitment to the library on the

Princeton campus; (2) Princeton's strong liberal arts tradition, which relies heavily on library resources, with leading programs in the sciences and humanities; and (3) significant externally funded research activity, which necessitates a knowledgeable and responsive library staff and a strong, comprehensive library collection.

All library operations are under a single administration. The libraries have a professional staff of 97 FTE and a support staff of 227 FTE. Including student labor, total staff size is 382 FTE (*ARL Statistics, 1983-84*, Washington, D.C., Association of Research Libraries, 1985).

The university librarian, Donald Koepp, has been in his current position for six years. Prior to his coming to Princeton, Dr. Koepp's experience had been with public institutions, including Arizona State University, Humboldt State University, and the University of California at Berkeley.

Sources of Funds and Levels of Expenditures

Exhibit I indicates the sources of funds and levels of expenditures for Princeton University for FY 1983-84. Exhibit II provides some key comparative statistics, including expenditure data, for the Princeton University Library.

In reviewing Princeton's sources of revenue, it is significant that one of the largest components of revenue is endowment income. In terms of endowment size Princeton ranks third in the nation, behind Harvard University and the University of Texas System. Total endowment for Princeton was $1,287,900,000 as of June 30, 1984 (1984 NACUBO *Comparative Performance Study*).

According to Princeton's financial vice president and treasurer, "the university's combined income from annual giving and from endowment almost precisely equals income from all tuition revenues. If income from these gifts (past and present) were to fail to keep pace with rising costs, tuition would have to rise twice as fast just to maintain existing program levels." (*A Campaign for Princeton*, p. 45).

In order to maintain and enhance this vital source of support, Princeton currently is engaged in a major fund-raising effort, *A Campaign for Princeton*. As of July 1, 1984, the campaign had raised $225.4 million or 68 percent of the $330 million goal. The campaign has provided critically needed support for many essential university activities. For example, it already has generated approximately $45 million in permanent endowment funds for professorships, student aid, and more general programmatic support. Most of these activities would have to be supported by general university funds (including tuition revenues) if

Princeton University

the new endowment funds were not available.

A Campaign for Princeton seeks $17,200,000 to expand and renovate parts of the Firestone Library, to create a new Near Eastern studies library that would consolidate one of Princeton's great collections, and to establish a new chemistry/biochemistry library. In addition, the campaign is seeking $8,000,000 for library materials, conservation, and new technology.

EXHIBIT I

University of Princeton Finances

Operating Budget*

	Total	Surplus
1983-84	$307,297,000	$54,000
1984-85**	332,935,000	3,000

*The total operating budget for 1984-85 includes $135 million for sponsored research at the Plasma Physics Laboratory. This amount, which represents 42 percent of the University's overall budget, increased by $10 million over the previous year.
**Projected

Income and Expenditures, 1983-84
(Excluding PPL)

Income

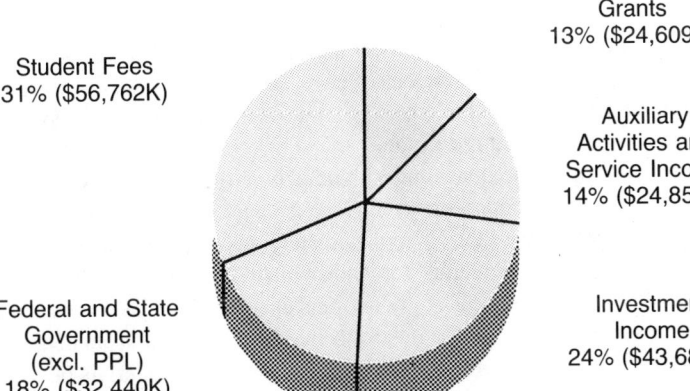

Gifts and Grants
13% ($24,609K)

Student Fees
31% ($56,762K)

Auxiliary Activities and Service Income
14% ($24,857K)

Federal and State Government
(excl. PPL)
18% ($32,440K)

Investment Income
24% ($43,683K)

EXHIBIT I *(continued)*

University of Princeton
Finances

Expenditures

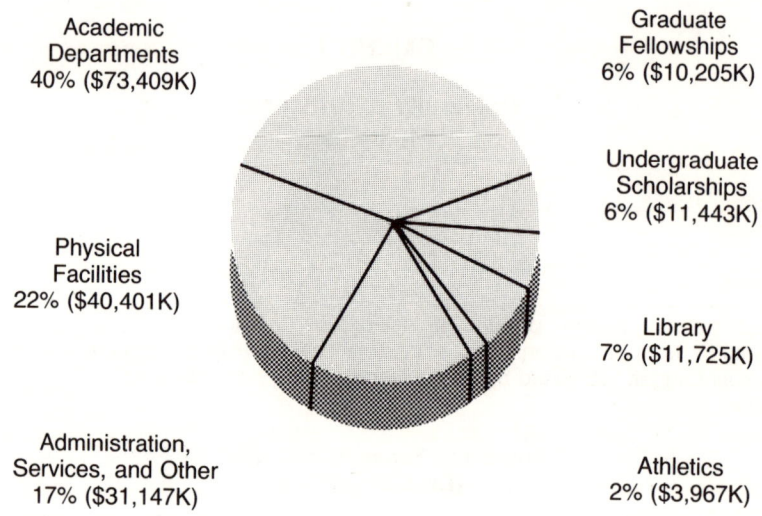

Academic Departments
40% ($73,409K)

Physical Facilities
22% ($40,401K)

Administration, Services, and Other
17% ($31,147K)

Graduate Fellowships
6% ($10,205K)

Undergraduate Scholarships
6% ($11,443K)

Library
7% ($11,725K)

Athletics
2% ($3,967K)

All development and fund-raising activities are handled centrally at Princeton. The university librarian serves as a resource person for the development office. In this role, he may meet with potential donors who have an interest in the library.

It is also important that approximately half the library's materials budget comes from endowment. In recent years the materials budget has been growing at a rate of approximately 10 percent a year. Since there are competing demands for endowment income other than the library, and since a portion of endowment income must be reinvested, this means that a portion of the materials budget must come from general university funds. As a consequence, the portion of the materials budget coming from general funds has been increasing at a rate greater than 10 percent.

Princeton University

EXHIBIT II

Library Comparative Summaries

	1979/80	1980/81	1981/82	1982/83	1983/84
Growth of the Collection					
Printed volumes	88,158	73,808	66,960	95,131	118,899[1]
Microtext units	106,264	47,514	78,435	62,595	81,357[1]
Serial Titles Currently Received	30,231	31,268	30,927	32,910	39,361[2]
Circulation					
Circulation Desk	279,977	241,894	213,570	287,622	284,239
Reserve Desk	126,764	135,087	216,517	193,817	181,678
Special Collections	283,834	274,654	209,664	235,928	247,626
Total Circulation	690,575	651,635	639,751	717,367	713,543
Expenditures					
Salaries & Wages[3]	$5,084,040	$5,435,049	$5,900,377	$6,625,815	$7,204,696
Books & Periodicals	2,588,531	2,803,550	2,810,186	3,171,448	3,413,791
Binding	151,438	175,238	215,266	250,618	327,421
Other operating expenses	373,328	377,973	722,282	725,115	930,883[4]
Special projects	362,065	607,390	487,420	269,294	424,214
Total Expenditures	$8,559,402	$9,399,200	$10,135,531	$11,042,290	$12,301,005
Interlibrary Loans					
Borrowed	3,963	3,267	4,033	4,360	5,280
Loaned	11,014	11,250	8,072	7,907	7,886

[1] Includes uncataloged documents and reverse duplicates.
[2] Includes for the first time 6,701 booksets.
[3] Includes benefits.
[4] Does not include Archives and Photoservices.

PLANNING AND MANAGEMENT PROCESSES

To better understand the library's role within the context of Princeton's overall planning and management processes, interviews were conducted with key institutional and library administrators. Project staff met with the provost, university librarian, controller, vice provost, and the computer center director.

Organizational Structure

In order to understand reporting relationships and decision making at Princeton, it is important to note that Princeton is truly a community of scholars. Senior administrators, when interviewed, frequently commented that at Princeton, scholarship and teaching are integrated under a single faculty. Distinguished faculty teach both undergraduates and graduates and it is not unusual for students to play an active role in research. Both president and provost are faculty members and the major administrative body at Princeton is the Council of the Princeton University Community (CPUC). Faculty involvement in the decision-making process at Princeton is considered the norm and not the exception.

In terms of the institution's day-to-day operations, two groups provide guidance to the president. First is the president's cabinet which meets weekly, primarily to address nonacademic issues. The cabinet includes all university vice presidents, including the financial vice president and treasurer, the vice presidents for development and for administrative affairs, and the university general counsel. The second presidential advisory group is the president's council, which is much broader in composition than the cabinet and includes the university librarian. The council meets monthly and serves as a mechanism for keeping the university community informed of major institutional developments; it also provides a forum for discussions of operational and academic issues. University advisory committees, such as the priorities committee, are also an integral part of decision making at Princeton. The roles of these committees are described later in this section.

To understand the governance structure at Princeton, it is important to understand the role of the provost. This position was established in 1967 and the provost is both chief academic officer and budget officer of the institution. In these roles, the provost has a tripartite function. First, as an operational officer he is responsible for overseeing library operations, the computer center, and the registrar. (The vice president for facilities, whose areas include physical plant, food services, and housing, also reports to the provost.) Second, the provost serves as senior planning and budget officer for the institution, and his third role is chief advisor and assistant to the president in addressing universitywide issues. For example, the provost recently chaired a special faculty committee on computing.

In exercising his responsibilities, the provost receives guidance from various advisory groups and committees. On a weekly basis, for example, the provost meets with faculty deans of colleges and graduate schools, as well as with the chairman of the University Research Board. In addition, the provost serves as chairman of the priorities committee, which has responsibility for developing the institution's budget and advising the president on budgetary matters.

The university librarian reports directly to the provost. As a consequence, the provost meets regularly with the university librarian—approximately every two weeks—to review and discuss library operations. Interviews with the university librarian indicated that the meetings are valuable in two ways: first, they keep the provost informed of library issues and second, they provide guidance to the university librarian as to whether plans and operations of the library are meeting user needs and are in line with institutional priorities.

The university librarian works with assistant librarians in addressing specific operational and policy issues; they are assisted by various advisory committees, composed of faculty, staff, and students with specific expertise and/or interest in library concerns. The principal advisory group to the library is the faculty library committee, which is chaired by the university librarian.

Management Processes

To understand the role of the Princeton University library within the planning, budgeting, and other management processes at Princeton, it is first necessary to consider how these processes work at the institutional level. Of major importance is the involvement of representatives of the Princeton University community in various key advisory committees. These committees play an active role in developing the university budget; in curriculum decisions, such as whether to add a new academic program; in reviewing key policy questions, such as the role of computers on campus; in working with the administration in establishing long-range goals and objectives, as in planning for major fund-raising efforts; and in examining sources of revenue to meet campus needs. All of the committees are under the purview of the Council of the Princeton University Community (CPUC).

In the sections that follow, four principal management functions at

Princeton and their role within the library are examined. These functions include planning, budgeting, implementation and control, and evaluation.

Planning

The planning process at Princeton takes place in three ways. First, the priorities committee, as part of its role in developing the budget, routinely examines future trends of significant factors that can affect both expenditure levels and revenue flow. Among factors considered by the committee are: projected levels of federal support and grant and contract activity; rates of inflation, both CPI and HEPI; and alternative income sources, such as earnings on endowment and tuition and fee revenue. If unfavorable trends are detected, the committee, with assistance from senior administrative staff and advice from unit heads, proposes corrective actions to address the problem.

A second way in which planning takes place at Princeton is through unit involvement in fund-raising activities. Recently, this process was employed in planning Princeton's current fund-raising effort: *A Campaign for Princeton*. In this instance, units requested funds for addressing priority areas within their operations. During consultations with the provost and other senior administrators, and as a result of interaction among units, these requests were distilled into a formal list of needs for the university as a whole. This list provided the foundation for developing *A Campaign for Princeton*.

A third component of the Princeton planning process involves ongoing interaction between unit heads and the provost. In weekly meetings of the dean's group and in individual consultations with unit heads, the provost receives advice on future programs, which enables him to develop a plan for all academic and support units under his control.

With regard to the library, plans are developed on two levels. First, through advisory committees, such as the faculty committee on the library, the university librarian can keep the university community informed of current and future issues affecting library operations. In addition, he can obtain feedback on constituent plans and priorities. Also, within the library, the librarian meets regularly with assistant librarians to discuss current issues and to formulate plans for the future.

On a second level, the university librarian meets with the provost on a regular basis to discuss current library operations and future plans. He also presents the budget to the priorities committee and discusses significant issues with this group, including concerns such as preservation of library materials and library automation. In addition, the librarian works with the development office on future fund-raising plans for the library.

Budgeting

As is true of the planning process, the budgetary process at Princeton is characterized by constituent involvement. Actual development of the university budget is a responsibility of the university's priorities committee.

The priorities committee is one of six charter committees of the Council of the Princeton University Community. As stipulated in the CPUC charter, the committee has sixteen regular members: three administrative officers serving ex-officio (the provost, who chairs the committee, the dean of the faculty, and the financial vice president and treasurer); six faculty members, including at least one from each of the four academic divisions and at least one nontenured member; four undergraduate students; two graduate students; and one representative of other groups on the Council (the administrative staff in the case of the 1985-86 committee).

The priorities committee advises the president on matters that affect preparation of the budget for the succeeding fiscal year and on longer-range plans for resource allocation. The committee's role is advisory and the weight given by the president and the governing board to its report depends on the persuasiveness of arguments presented and on the quality of final recommendations. The committee has neither the time nor expertise for undertaking a line-by-line review of the entire university budget or involving itself in day-to-day management of the university. Actual allocation of funds within major budgetary units is, therefore, left to university officers responsible for those units. The committee's role is, instead, to make recommendations that establish, in broad terms, priorities that govern use of university resources.

The rationale behind establishing the priorities committee provides an excellent example of why constituent involvement is so important to decision making at Princeton. In *Budgeting and Resource Allocation at Princeton University* (1972), the major reasons cited for constituent participation on the committee were: (1) that difficult resource allocation decisions require a broad range of informed judgment and opinion and (2) that if retrenchment or reallocation is necessary, broader participation in the decision-making process would "lead to more widespread understanding of both the choices before us and the decisions reached." During interviews with institutional administrators, two additional factors became apparent. First, the committee is a mechanism for linking those charged with preparing the budget to those charged with implementing it. Second, the involvement of academic representatives on the committee enhances the credibility of the budget process within the university community as a whole.

Procedurally, the priorities committee begins meeting regularly in October and continues to meet approximately twice a week until Christmas vacation. October and November sessions are devoted mainly to reviewing requests from individual budgetary units, and evaluating both the needs in those units and the possibility of deferring requests or making budget reductions. To assist in this process, university officers responsible for major budgetary units prepare written budget reports for the committee and then meet with the committee to discuss them. Presentations are made on discrete components of the budget, such as faculty staffing, computing, facilities, and the library.

The university librarian is one of the officers who meet with the priorities committee. His presentation does not encompass all budgetary elements, such as salaries, supplies, and travel, related to library operations. Rather, it focuses on items such as acquisitions, which pertain to the library as a university resource. The rising cost of library materials, for example, is a major concern of the priorities committee. Normally, the committee reaches no firm conclusions during initial budget presentations, but waits until all individual budgets have been reviewed before making any recommendations.

The committee believes it important to maintain communication with the rest of the university community. It therefore continually seeks the views of that community, both on specific budgetary problems and on more general priorities for the university. To facilitate communication, written budgetary presentations prepared for the committee also are made available to the campus press and to the general university community. The committee also provides progress reports throughout the fall to the CPUC and other groups and, through *The Daily Princetonian* and other channels of communication, to the wider university community.

In December, initial budget projections are made for the entire budget period, including a re-estimation of all those components that are not under direct university control. The rest of that month is devoted to a further examination and discussion of individual budgetary units, during which time an effort is made to determine where reductions can be sustained or where increases seem absolutely essential. The objective of this process is to develop recommendations—for tuition and other charges as well as for major categories of expenditures—that can be expected to produce a balanced budget for the upcoming budget period. Results of these discussions are reported by the provost to the CPUC just before the holiday recess. The committee then reassembles in early

January to review its tentative recommendations in the context of a set of four-year budget projections, which, with their implications, are incorporated into its final report.

While the priorities committee is developing its budget recommendations, another committee, the resources committee, is examining revenue components of the budget. The financial vice president, who is the treasurer, chairs this committee and is an ex-officio member of the priorities committee.

Following budget hearings and detailed deliberations, the priorities committee submits its budget recommendations to the president in early spring. The president then presents his recommendations to the university board of trustees. The board's finance committee reviews the president's recommendations and presents its findings to the board. In late spring, the board formally approves a budget for the coming fiscal year. The component of the budget dealing with capital equipment needs is prepared by the central administration and then submitted to the board for approval.

Implementation and Control

While the priorities committee has responsibility for developing the university budget, the controller's office is responsible for the preparation of the actual budget document, budget analysis, and control. The controller's office is also responsible for reconciling budget data to the financial accounting systems of the institution. All the technical aspects of the budgetary process are quite centralized.

Budget control at Princeton focuses primarily on aggregate unit budgets rather than on specific items within these budgets, such as travel or supplies. As a result, institutional units, such as the library, have some flexibility in moving funds among budget items. However, the budget office issues monthly reports and analyzes variances to insure that budgets are administered in a manner that is consistent with overall institutional goals and objectives. In this regard, the focus of budget control at Princeton is on post-audit rather than pre-audit accountability. If expenditure patterns, for example, are consistently out of line with the budget, the unit head must justify these patterns or run the risk of having funds reallocated to other units in subsequent fiscal years.

Within the library, the assistant librarian for administrative services is responsible for budget control and implementation. While the university librarian can move funds among budget categories, the acquisitions budget is not reallocable. However, permanent salary savings, i.e., from lapsed positions, have been used to fund operating costs of the library's automated systems. Funding requirements of these systems have been significant. In 1974-75, the library spent $24,000 on automation; in 1980-81, it spent $276,000. The comparable figure for 1983-84 was $468,000 (*Report of the University Librarian for 1983-84*).

Evaluation

At the institutional level, academic and support programs are evaluated in a number of ways. Advisory committees, such as the faculty library committee, review specific functional areas on an ongoing basis. In addition, the priorities committee reviews both operational performance and resource needs during its annual budget hearings with university officers responsible for major budgetary units. Program review is also an ongoing component of management processes at Princeton.

Management Style

Princeton's administration fosters the concept of participatory decision making. While technical aspects of budgeting and control are handled centrally, policy decisions are made on a more distributed basis. As a consequence, constituent involvement in the management of Princeton engenders an attitude that, if difficult decisions are to be made responsibly, it is imperative that all parties involved understand the rationale underlying these decisions and the consequences associated with their implementation.

Concerning the library, constituent involvement in operation and policy decisions insures that users' needs are met and that the university community understands the challenges facing the library. For example, that preservation of library materials is recognized as a serious problem by the university community results from the university librarian's ability to articulate his concerns to a broad audience.

The university librarian, when faced with an administrative or policy issue, first thoroughly researches the issue and then seeks counsel from both his staff and representatives of the university community. Such consultation tends to yield decisions that are supported by facts and responsive to all concerned.

RESPONDING TO TECHNOLOGICAL CHANGE

Philosophy on Library Automation

The approach taken by the Princeton University library towards automation was first stated by former university librarian William S. Dix in his annual report for 1965-66. Dr. Dix indicated there that the Princeton University library was not a good site for experimentation. Thus, he recommended that Princeton should wait until proven systems were available elsewhere and then apply them with vigor to the university library. He assumed that such systems would be developed by other libraries.

A Conceptual Framework

The current university librarian, Donald Koepp, in his 1983-84 annual report on the library, described development of automated library systems on the Princeton campus in terms of three generations. According to Dr. Koepp, the first generation of automated systems consisted of nationwide library networks, such as OCLC or RLG, and local systems that performed simple processes—such as automated circulation systems—which were better handled locally than through national networks. The second generation of automated library systems involved development of online public access catalogs (OPAC) and the third generation included development of local area networks or LANs. In this case, use of LANs involved distribution of exceedingly powerful computing equipment to faculty and students and linked computer "work stations" to local computer networks. With regard to future configuration of such networks, Dr. Koepp noted that:

> The economics of computing capacity versus the economics of data transmission over long distances will radically change the nature of today's networks. Princeton today has twenty-seven terminals connected by leased telephone lines to the Research Libraries Group's IBM 3081 computer in Stanford, California. In five years that number will probably have declined considerably. However, all of the 40 to 60 million bibliographic records, by then in the RLG database, will be maintained locally on member library campuses and will be updated periodically, perhaps weekly, by mailings of tapes of the updated database to all member libraries.
>
> The major problem which the owner members of RLG will then face is assuring that the database is kept up to date. Each of the members will have to supply RLG with records of the cataloging done in their library, which will update the RLG computer.

In summary, Dr. Koepp believes that the three generations of library computing, however mixed because of differential development within research libraries, are clearly a succession of major steps, each dependent on developments in computing equipment and software and each requiring major adjustment for library users and staffs. And each, it should be added, carrying its own price tag.

University Libraries in Transition

History of Automation at the Princeton University Library

Within the context of the conceptual structure described above, the history of automated library systems at the Princeton University library has been as follows:

First Generation

The Princeton University library has used three nationwide library networks: PURRS, OCLC, and RLIN. It has also used three *local automated systems*: 3M, GEAC, and ISIS.

Nationwide Library Networks

PURRS. Starting in 1975, Princeton University librarians who previously had received training for searching commercial and governmental databases began to provide this service within the library. The first formal system, PURRS (or Princeton University Reference and Referral Service), grew rapidly from its first use in the engineering library in 1975. In 1977, in various library locations, eight searchers spent an estimated 28 hours of time on online connection with the approximately 23 databases available worldwide to Princeton at that time. By 1981, 14 librarians were spending a total of more than 300 hours mining for 800 users the enormous resources then available to them worldwide in an estimated 110 databases.

PURRS' most rapid growth occurred in the years 1975-81. By the end of 1981, this type of bibliographic searching had become an integral part of library reference service and focus had shifted to maintaining the level of service and keeping abreast of new developments, a focus that continues to this day.

OCLC. The twin developments of large database technology and improved hardware reliability provided the tools by which library consortia could develop. The first of these, the Ohio College Library Center, was developed in 1968. OCLC was an interactive nationwide computer network that permitted libraries to use finished cataloging done by other libraries, including the Library of Congress, as well as to contribute their own original cataloging, which could then be used by others. It presumed that most libraries would maintain separate catalogs of their own local holdings. As a consequence, computer-produced file cards were made available to members for card catalogs.

By 1974, OCLC had 300 members. In addition to providing extremely

Princeton University

quick access to all Roman language cataloging done by the Library of Congress, OCLC had developed a cataloging database, contributed by other libraries, that appeared large enough to meet virtually all of Princeton's cataloging needs within a short time. According to the Princeton University librarian, however, during Princeton's use of OCLC between 1974 and 1980, the library's cataloging staff never was able to glean anything approaching all its cataloging from the system.

The extraordinary variety of standards in cataloging in the OCLC database reflected the wide range in size, sophistication, and purpose of OCLC-member libraries. Because of this range, many records were not sufficiently full or accurate to use in research library catalogs. This resulted from a structural arrangement in OCLC, by which the basic record prepared by the first library to catalog a book became the permanent master bibliographic record for that title in the database.* Consequently, the OCLC database contained the first, rather than best, cataloging of a title, which was exasperating for Princeton. While a title's original file cards might meet the first library's standards, they might be inadequate for Princeton's.

This is not to say that Princeton's use of OCLC was not successful. Such use did result in an enormous amount of derived cataloging, and it eliminated the costly and burdensome local manufacture of catalog cards. The current university librarian, however, feels that the inherent limitations of the OCLC system set boundaries on its use as an online system, and at Princeton it was used essentially as a typewriter of catalog cards. Furthermore, the librarian believes that:

> participation in OCLC failed to familiarize even cataloging staff with the opportunities and rigors of online processing and network processing of library bibliographic records. "Routinizing" the current revolution in on-line library processing and access to records would come later, with RLIN in 1980 and with GEAC in 1981.

RLIN. A consortium called the Research Libraries Group (RLG) was established in 1974, composed of Columbia, Yale, Harvard, and the New York Public Library. RLG members joined to work on difficult library problems that they felt could be addressed more effectively as a group. The consortium had four programs: Shared Collection Development; Shared Resources; Preservation of Library Resources; and an underlying bibliographic network similar to OCLC, called RLIN (Research Libraries Information Network). In 1978, RLIN was adopted by Princeton as the automated system to be used. Shortly before this,

---

* An exception would be cataloging provided by the Library of Congress, which would appear in the database as a duplicate record.

Harvard had dropped out of the consortium and was replaced by Stanford.

Princeton joined RLG in March 1979 for several reasons, including access to the RLIN cataloging system and because of the potential for using other automated processing systems developed through RLIN. Transition from OCLC to RLIN cataloging was relatively simple and Princeton rapidly moved into a position of leadership among RLG institutions in using the system.

According to the university librarian, RLIN provided the library with access to records for all books cataloged by other members of RLG, which shared Princeton cataloging standards. Because of Princeton's participation in RLG, the manner in which the university catalogs books and the ways in which it provides reference service and selects books, as well as its interlibrary loan capabilities, all have changed profoundly.

More important for the future of library automation at Princeton was RLIN's providing the library with its first approximation of an online catalog, albeit one not intended for public use. Furthermore, although RLIN was too expensive to provide unlimited terminals and unlimited searching capability, its presence in the library provided an opportunity for educating staff in computing techniques they would need to provide high quality library service in the future. Thus, internal use of the system gave library staff a basis for understanding requirements of a real online, public-access catalog.

Local Automated Systems

3M. In 1977 the library departed radically from its original philosophy of using only tested systems; it entered into an agreement with the 3M Company for the installation of a new computer-controlled circulation system for both the main circulation desk and the reserve desk. The campus community had short notice that this event was about to occur and little time was provided for staff training. Certainly no efforts were made to provide machine-readable bibliographic records of library holdings before the system was installed, although the existence of such records would have simplified the process of circulating books through the system.

The 3M system worked reasonably well during the summer of 1977, but by midfall of that year it was evident that the system was not meeting expectations. In addition to apparent inadequacies in hardware, programming for the system was being refined continually during the entire period it was in place. Problems also resulted from the absence of previously established bibliographic records, all of which had to be created each time a book circulated for the first time. Because of these problems, the staff never became fully familiar with the system.

The 3M system finally was removed in May 1978 and circulation procedures reverted to a manual process. However, a small portion of the system was retained and used in the campus computer for processing reserve books. Although the university incurred no financial costs associated with the system, due to the foresight of university counsel in drawing up the contract, the 3M experiment was costly in terms of massive inconvenience to library users and disenchantment of library staff.

Both service and cost concerns, however, led to a continued investigation of the application of computing to library circulation control. One cause for the failure of the 3M system—the absence of any bibliographic records for books that were to circulate—led to reinstallation of a computer to develop a database for those books the library could assume would circulate heavily. The chosen computer and software were offered by one of two companies that seemed to have systems which, with some further development, might meet library needs. By early spring of 1980, this database development effort resulted in the presence of some 100,000 records in a computer file, from which they could be recalled and displayed on a terminal; the matching books were bar-coded.

GEAC. In June 1981, following tests that determined that a large percentage of books which would circulate had been bar-coded, use of the GEAC circulation control system began at the Firestone circulation desk. By year-end, the system had worked so well that plans were underway to extend its use to the reserve room. The library also was considering other applications for the system, including the degree to which it could be used as an online catalog.

ISIS and Purely Local Systems. From 1974 through 1981 there were several attempts to provide information locally that was not (and in some cases is still not) available through traditional bibliographic means, whether through the card catalog or commercially available indexes. These projects were generally small databases developed by local programmers using central computing facilities. The databases themselves were often of transitory interest. Experience with these systems, however, was invaluable to library staff, in that it provided them with orientation and training necessary for implementation and maintenance of the large database production systems of GEAC and RLIN.

In terms of other locally created databases, the library, in July 1980, issued the first edition of a list by account numbers of approximately 30,000 serials to which the library then subscribed. This database subsequently has been updated regularly.

In addition, a federal grant in 1978 enabled the library to work systematically on the very large arrearage of uncataloged literary manuscripts stored under very little control in the Rare Books and Special Collections Department. Because of the slowness with which conventional manuscript cataloging takes place, the library developed a process for indexing manuscripts using ISIS, a series of computer programs developed and maintained by UNESCO and its own computer center and geared toward small- and medium-sized databases. Since the adoption of ISIS, indexing has proceeded more rapidly, although it will be many years, even with additional outside funding, before all of Princeton's literary manuscripts are fully under control.

Second Generation (Online Public Access Catalog)

Over the last two years, two library task forces studied the library's position with regard to acquiring an Online Public Access Catalog (OPAC). The focus of these task forces was decidedly different: one group was charged with assessing capabilities of systems currently being sold, while the other group addressed implications of switching to an online catalog for technical processing functions. However, their conclusions were identical: that for several reasons, the Princeton University library was not prepared at that time to make a move such as adopting an OPAC. The premise underlying this decision was:

> We would not wish to settle for an online catalog which would do less for us than does our current card catalog. There is currently no commercially available system with proven performance which offers the features we need to replace our card catalog. Expensive though the card catalog is to maintain, even with the inadequacies occasioned by the slow process of producing and filing cards and the lack of keyword searching, at least potentially available in an online catalog, the card catalog, as maintained in our library, is functioning sufficiently well to preclude the need for an immediate change.

Despite concerns over the feasibility of an online catalog, the library engaged in a three-month functional test of the Carlyle online catalog system in spring 1985. The Carlyle system is a relatively new turnkey product that is presently in use at three other U.S. locations: Rice University, the University of Miami, and the New York Public Library.

The system appears to be economically attractive and the three-month trial period was intended to provide sufficient information for evaluating it. During the test period, library patrons were free to use the system and forms were available for user comments. In addition, over two-thirds of the library's professional staff alternated in staffing a "help" desk. They kept a log of problems and responded to user inquiries.

Through their involvement in the test phase, staff became familiar with and proficient in using the system.

The Carlyle and GEAC system at Princeton are not linked, so that a patron who finds a book in Carlyle has to use a GEAC terminal to determine whether or not it has been checked out. While the Carlyle system provides author, title, and subject information, the GEAC system supplies only the author, title, call number, and circulation status. Since the GEAC circulation system indicates only what has been checked out and the Carlyle system has only a limited number of records, a patron still must refer to the card catalog for older materials that are not on either system. For example, there may be books in the Firestone library stacks that have not been checked out since the implementation of GEAC and which, as a result, have no circulation record in GEAC. Also, the branch libraries are generally not on the GEAC system. The library, however, is in the process of expanding the automated circulation system to the branches. The current automated systems, therefore, supplement the card catalog, but do not replace it.

In terms of user satisfaction with the Carlyle system, an editorial in the *Daily Princetonian* (April 3, 1985) noted that:

> The new Carlyle system, which serves as an electronic card catalog, has already proven to be a useful and easily accessible addition to the GEAC system at Firestone. It provides a quick and painless way of finding research information which might otherwise be overlooked amid the clutter of millions of catalog cards.
>
> While it may have its faults, such as an inability to identify whether or not a book is in the library, the recent change illustrates the advantages of greater computerization of the entire library system. The university should definitely continue keeping the card catalogue "on line" and increasing the number of terminals available to students, if not with the Carlyle system, then with a similar one.

The library has since worked out a lease arrangement with Carlyle for 18 months. The university librarian indicated that use of the Carlyle system may help solve algorithm problems that they have experienced. It also may increase database capacity by bringing the number of records in the system up to 250,000. Under the lease arrangement, the library pays maintenance costs for the system and has the option to purchase both software and equipment if it chooses to do so.

Third Generation (Local Area Networks)

A movement towards a third generation of library systems is being developed at Princeton. In March 1984, a special faculty committee on computing at Princeton was established to recommend general guidelines for developing computing plans. A preliminary report of the committee issued in March 1985 indicated that Princeton should:

> Continue to plan and implement a distributed network of computing resources, including clusters of micro-computers, larger computers and other specialized resources operated centrally, and a hierarchical system of communication networks to tie these resources together. Our most important recommendation in this area is that the university begin immediately to study the alternative approaches to a campuswide "trunk" network, so that planning for local networks and computer clusters can proceed with an ability to connect to that system as one of the design criteria.

The library certainly would be an integral part of such a network. Furthermore, the committee, in describing its proposed system, cited the branch library model as the paradigm for a distributed computer system. Under this model, staff and other resources are budgeted and administered centrally but work closely with users in providing technical assistance and advice on computer-related applications.

With regard to the administration of institutional computer resources, the special faculty committee on computing proposed the following:

> That the current administrative structures for computing be reviewed and revised to serve better the needs of this new computing environment. In particular, we recommend that a new senior administrative position be created to oversee all campus computing activities and that a standing faculty committee on university computing be established to assist in that effort.

In fall 1985, a vice president for computing was appointed.

Current Status of Library Automation at Princeton

Cataloging (Uses of RLIN and GEAC). Because of its commitment to scholarship and to meet the needs of the Princeton University community, the library continues to do substantial original cataloging. It contributes cataloging copy to the RLG database, which now contains about 20 million records. Approximately 250,000 of these represent books belonging to Princeton. About 45,000 records were contributed by Princeton in the process of creating cataloging that meets national standards for books that previously were not in RLIN.

The library also uses the RLG database to derive cataloging copy contributed by other RLG members. In 1983-84 this accounted for almost one-quarter of its cataloging production. Because the shared database contains all cataloging done by the Library of Congress, which serves as Princeton's standard, the library was able to introduce an exciting new processing change in 1985. By cataloging online all books (for which there is Library of Congress cataloging copy) at time of receipt, the library was able to cut processing time to an absolute minimum. Fully 25 percent of books received in 1983-84 were cataloged and on the shelf within 48 hours of their arrival in the library, and this percentage was expected to reach one-third by 1984-85. (It is not possible for catalog cards to be in place nearly so quickly, although the online RLIN catalog record is complete.)

Another benefit of an online network is the ability to share projects intended to make the database more useful. Princeton, for example, has participated in a project with several other RLG members to convert cataloging records for their master negative microfilm collection to machine-readable form to load those records into RLIN. The RLG program goals of preservation and shared collection development were linked in this project, and needs of scholarship greatly served by the addition of 25,000 records to the RLG database (from which a listing has been formed) making it available to non-RLG members as well. Princeton contributed 1,900 of these records.

Acquisitions. In 1982, Princeton implemented the RLIN acquisition system, which represented the library's first attempt at automating its ordering process. In 1983-84, for reasons that included cost and efficiency, the library replaced the RLIN system with the GEAC acquisitions system. The selection of the GEAC system was based on the library's prior experience with the company and on the fact that the system could interface with equipment and resources already in place.

One feature of the GEAC acquisitions system not available in the RLIN acquisitions system made it extremely attractive to the library: it supported a rigorous fiscal system that would allow the library to keep, for the first time, accurate and detailed records of some 70 book accounts.

Another feature of the GEAC system was its capacity for automated serials check-in, a process by which some 300,000 individual issues of newspapers, magazines, journals, monographs in series, and other serial publications that are received by subscription each year are checked into the library, claimed when not received as scheduled, and otherwise accounted for. Currently this is a completely manual operation. For individual items destined for branch libraries, the process is repeated by staff in those locations because they currently do not have access to the central record. Clearly this is a very labor-intensive operation, and it has been a top priority of the library's technical services department to find an automated system that made sense in the Princeton environment. The automation of serials check-in is expected to result in salary savings to support operating costs.

The university librarian indicated that use of the GEAC acquisitions system should yield significant cost savings for the library. In addition, use of the system is in line with RLG's policy of decentralizing those activities that are not essentially shared in order to reduce the workload of RLIN and to minimize member communication costs.

Improved Service. The university librarian believes that implementation of the GEAC system has resulted in improved library service. In 1982, for example, the library automated its reserve service. The reserve component of the GEAC system involves both circulation of books and placement of books on reserve, including the creation of lists of items on reserve for particular courses for use by both faculty and students of the courses. Although queues still exist from time to time in the reserve room, they are usually a result of limited counter space and the time necessary to page requested books.

At the circulation desk, the automatic recall system has been a major improvement. While it always has been possible to recall a book, the automatic system tracks whether, as a result of the recall, the book actually was returned. This operation could not be as effective if done manually because of the sheer volume of books involved.

In addition, during the last two years, the library has begun to use GEAC as an in-process control system. This is a very expensive service to maintain because each and every book in process—and there are sometimes up to 20,000 of them—must be charged out from work station to station. However, for the first time in its history the library can actually locate the in-process books that are requested by its readers.

Not the least of improvements wrought by GEAC was the capability to produce reports based on data buried within the circulation database. For the last year the library has regularly produced lists of books reported missing, of books that circulated more than a certain number of times, and of books held for another reader or recalled more than a certain number of times—all for selector's review. None of this information could have been gleaned systematically during prior years of manual operations.

As noted earlier, the library is in the process of extending the GEAC circulation system to locations that maintain their own circulation records. The intent is to provide a record for every book in the collection, with the hope of providing bibliographic access for those branches whose collections share subject interest, but currently do not have access to those books that exist in collections other than their own. Towards this end, each record, though not as complete as the corresponding card catalog record, will contain more than the minimum information necessary to identify a book. It should be noted that these goals are rather different from those of the Firestone use of the system, in that it is not possible to create a record for every book housed in Firestone. The GEAC record, therefore, will be created primarily for circulation and will not, in most cases, provide more than the bare minimum of access points.

Staff Requirements. As indicated in the section on management processes, funding for the majority of operating costs associated with automated library systems has come from salary savings. Processing under these systems, however, has required a more sophisticated technical knowledge on the part of library personnel. In recognition of this fact, 38 support-staff processing positions (out of 70 audited positions) have been reclassified. In 1981 only a small number of staff were proficient in the use of RLIN or GEAC, and very few were competent in both. Currently all processing staff and most public service librarians use RLIN or GEAC; more than half use both. In 1981-82 the reference department reported 538 RLIN uses. Almost half that number was reported in 1983-84 in Princeton's Woodrow Wilson School library alone.

In addition, maintenance of two large-scale production systems—updating documentation, training, planning, installing, and repairing—has grown to the extent that in 1983-84 the library created a position for an automated systems planner/coordinator. This person is responsible for centralizing certain functions and for tasks formerly distributed among various staff members, and for formalizing the operation, maintenance, and continuing evaluation of the libraries' automated systems.

Relationship with the Computer Center. Services provided by the computer center to the library include technical assistance and peripheral support as needed, such as high-speed printing. The computer center also backs up the GEAC tapes. An assistant program manager currently devotes approximately one half-day per week to the library.

Integration of Systems. Since the library currently uses several different types of automated systems, the question of systems integration was raised during interviews with the university librarian, who indicated that a certain amount of redundancy could be beneficial. He noted, for example, that problems in one part of an integrated system can bring the entire system "down." Problems in non-integrated systems, however, tend to be unique to one system, thus leaving other systems unaffected and operational.

User Fees. Fees are charged only for remote database searching and are intended to cover only direct costs associated with the process. Access charges and borrowing fees also are charged to library patrons who are not members of the Princeton University community.

Retrospective Conversion. The faculty library committee does not

University Libraries in Transition

support retrospective conversion (a process in which manual records for other library materials are turned into machine- readable records) at this time because of cost and funding considerations. According to the university librarian, the philosophy at Princeton to date has been to "create as much cataloging of previously uncataloged material as possible, rather than to deploy staff time in recreating in machine-readable form records which already exist in the card catalog." This philosophy, however, may change with the advent of an online catalog.

SUMMARY

Development of automated library systems at Princeton has been shaped by two major factors. First, the participatory nature of the decision-making process at Princeton has led to user involvement in selecting and evaluating automated systems. Second, the tradition of scholarship and research at Princeton has led to a philosophy of not employing automated library systems merely for the sake of automation, but rather to use automation to make resources of the library available to library patrons in a more effective and efficient manner.

As noted in the section on management processes, Princeton is truly a community of scholars. This characteristic is mirrored in constituent involvement in both planning and budgeting. Within the context of a "single faculty," the library is the common link that ties the university community together. In support of this role, the university librarian is kept informed of institutional operations and priorities through his involvement on university advisory committees, such as the president's council and the faculty committee on the library (which he chairs). He also is able, in turn, to keep the university community informed of challenges and opportunities affecting the library. His effectiveness in this role is evident in that the preservation of library materials is considered a major issue by a significant part of the university community and that library automation is ranked as a priority item in current fund-raising efforts.

The library's automated system is perceived as a model for a universitywide distributed computer system. In acquiring automated systems, the library has been guided by a philosophy that such systems should enhance and improve traditional library services. To implement this philosophy, the library has used national networks such as RLIN to enhance its in-house capabilities and employed systems such as GEAC and Carlyle that interface effectively with traditional library procedures and systems.

In summary, the Princeton University library, due in large measure to the effective management style of the current university librarian, is very much in tune with management processes of the institution. Furthermore, the university librarian, through his active participation in these processes, has been able to foster an approach to library automation that is supported by the university community and that reinforces the role of the university library in the rich traditions of the Princeton University community.

UNIVERSITY OF ILLINOIS

"*Higher education is a high priority in the state, and this is reflected in strong support for statewide cooperative efforts involving academic and public libraries.*"
Hugh Atkinson
University Librarian

BACKGROUND

Institutional Profile

Chartered by the Illinois General Assembly in 1867 as the Illinois Industrial College, the University of Illinois has pursued the goals of instruction, research, and public service for more than one hundred years. There are two principal campuses, one in Urbana-Champaign and the other in Chicago. Cooperative efforts to provide universitywide services link the two campuses, although both fulfill their academic functions independently, with substantial delegated authority.

The flagship campus is the University of Illinois at Urbana-Champaign (UI-UC), an educational community of approximately 34,500 students and 11,500 faculty and staff. The older and larger of the two campuses, UI Urbana-Champaign, has 21 colleges and schools that offer undergraduate, graduate, and professional programs attended by students from the 50 states and the District of Columbia, as well as from 100 foreign countries. UI-UC is a comprehensive graduate and research institution whose strengths include the nation's largest public university library, superior computer facilities, and broad and diverse research programs. Its Cooperative Extension Service serves the state's 102 counties through a wide-reaching program delivery system. The university is also the home of several other statewide service agencies, such as the Small Homes-Building Research Council, Illinois State Geological Survey, Illinois Natural History Survey, and Illinois State Water Survey.

In recent rankings of U.S. university programs by various organizations, Urbana-Champaign was judged in the top 10 nationally in such areas as accounting, engineering, library science, agriculture, and education.

The other university campus, the University of Illinois at Chicago, was created in September 1982 by the merger of the former Chicago Circle and Medical Center campuses. The Chicago campus serves approximately 25,000 students and is the largest university in the Chicago area. Undergraduate, graduate, and professional programs in health sciences, humanities, fine arts, natural and social sciences, engineering, social work, education and business are offered in its 14 colleges and schools.

The university is governed by a board of trustees that formulates general policies. Nine of the twelve board members are elected. Two nonvoting student members are chosen by students at each campus, and the state governor is an ex-officio board member.

The University of Illinois is one of five Illinois state school systems.

———————————— University of Illinois ————————————

The other systems, including Southern Illinois University and Sangamon State, are smaller than the UI system. All five are coordinated by the Illinois State Board of Higher Education, which has curriculum approval as well as some influence in budget approval.

Library Profile

The University of Illinois library at Urbana-Champaign is the third largest academic library in the nation, with 6,615,550 volumes as of FY 1984. Total expenditures for FY 1984 were $13,586,014, of which $4,369,205 (32 percent) was spent on books, periodicals, and other research materials. A total of $7,454,359 (55 percent) was spent on salaries and wages. The staff, including student assistants, totals 543, with 120 professional and 295 technical and clerical employees. In FY 1984, library expenditures accounted for 3.4 percent of the university's educational and general expenditures, which totaled $405,363,913 *(ARL 1985 Statistics)*.

The Urbana-Champaign library is a decentralized system consisting of 39 departmental libraries and special collections. All library units on campus, including the law library, report to the university librarian. Not only does the library provide essential support to academic programs and research activities on the campuses, but it also is a major research and reference facility for the State of Illinois. As part of ILLINET, the cooperative lending network that supports primarily public libraries, it is one of four lending centers in the state. The UI library is also part of the statewide Library Computer System (LCS), an interlibrary online catalog retrieval system that links the university with 25 other academic libraries in the state.

Sources of Revenue

The state legislature makes one appropriation of $418 million to the University of Illinois, which has a total budget of approximately $1 billion. Other revenue sources include federal appropriations, federal grants and contracts, private gifts and grants, and indirect cost recoveries (ICRs). Income by revenue source and appropriations are shown in Exhibit I.

Library funds can be broken down into the following components by revenue source (figures are rough estimates):

1. $13 million from the university (including ICRs allocated to the library)

University Libraries in Transition

EXHIBIT I

University of Illinois

ESTIMATED INCOME, fiscal year ending June 30, 1985:		
State appropriations from tax revenue	$418,009,820	41.81%
Federal appropriations	16,541,000	1.65%
Student fees	77,413,300	7.74%
Other sponsored programs	18,448,000	1.85%
Private gifts and grants	14,902,000	1.49%
State contracts	14,570,000	1.46%
Federal grants and contracts	90,415,000	9.04%
Medical service plan	26,333,000	2.63%
Institutional costs recovered	55,612,397	5.56%
Earnings and miscellaneous	150,034,600	15.01%
Total educational and general income	$882,279,117	88.24%
Auxiliary enterprises—residence halls, student union buildings, etc.	103,924,000	10.39%
Gifts and endowment income for scholarships, etc.	13,681,000	1.37%
GRAND TOTAL, ESTIMATED INCOME	$999,884,117	100.00%
APPROPRIATIONS, fiscal year ending June 30, 1985:		
Instruction and departmental research	$215,573,470	21.56%
Independent operations	163,448,806	16.35%
Separately budgeted research	157,805,801	15.78%
Statewide extension and public services	70,836,528	7.08%
Academic support	71,862,361	7.19%
Student services	13,033,451	1.30%
Administration and general	62,997,854	6.30%
Retirement system	32,563,520	3.26%
Operation and maintenance of physical plant	92,300,106	9.23%
Refunds	5,000	.00%
Total educational and general appropriations	$880,426,897	88.05%
Auxiliary enterprises—residence halls, student union buildings, etc.	103,924,000	10.39%
Student aid	15,533,220	1.55%
GRAND TOTAL, APPROPRIATIONS	$999,884,117	100.00%
APPROPRIATIONS BY LOCATION, fiscal year ending June 30, 1985:		
Chicago		$462,194,708
Urbana-Champaign		491,559,497
Central administration		46,129,912
GRAND TOTAL, APPROPRIATIONS		$900,884,117

2. $350,000 from funds generated through interlibrary loans ($4 per loan)
3. $250,000 from funds authorized by the Higher Education Act, Title II-C (a program to build, catalog, and preserve collections of national stature)

4. $100,000 in other state grants
5. $60,000 in annual giving, primarily from a group known as the University of Illinois Library Friends

Indirect cost recoveries to all grants received by UI-UC are a revenue source. This amounted to $830,370 in FY 1985. From the ICR fund, $359,570 was budgeted for supplies and services, $30,000 for equipment, and $440,000 for library materials.

University librarian Hugh Atkinson has taken the initiative in trying to generate other sources of financial support for the library. Statewide cooperative arrangements are a major priority. As mentioned previously, the UI at Urbana-Champaign is one of four state library centers that form ILLINET, a cooperative lending network that primarily supports public libraries. Other centers are the Chicago Public Library, the State Library, and Southern Illinois University library at Carbondale.

The program is administered out of the State Library and is funded under the Library Services and Construction Act (LSCA) through the program for interlibrary cooperation. In its 17 years of operation, LSCA Title III has provided nearly $80 million to support institutional library networks through projects involving telecommunications, bibliographic access, interlibrary loans, and other resource-sharing activities. No charges are assessed for borrowing books, but each of the four reference centers receives $4 a transaction from state-administered grant funds each time a book is loaned.

Development Efforts. The university librarian also has been active in development efforts on behalf of the library. With partial funding from the $4-per-transaction reimbursement for interlibrary lending, the university librarian hired a director of development with whom he works closely to build support among alumni, academic departments, and other interested groups. Funds that are raised go directly to the University of Illinois Foundation and are used for various purposes, including expansion of special collections.

The university recently completed a successful five-year, capital *Campaign for Illinois*, which exceeded its original target of $100 million by almost one-third (total funds raised were $132 million). Plans are now underway for the campuses to strengthen their own development efforts and move toward constituent fund raising. Under this arrangement, the University of Illinois Foundation will function mainly as a coordinating body. Efforts during the recent capital campaign were focused on raising endowments. For the library, in particular, the goal was to raise a $5-million endowment for library materials. The goal has been partially met.

PLANNING AND MANAGEMENT PROCESSES

In order to better understand the management processes at the University of Illinois, the following administrators were interviewed:
System Level
- Vice President for Business and Finance and Comptroller
- Vice President for Academic Affairs
- Management Analyst (involved in development and operation of the statewide LCS system)

Campus Level (Urbana-Champaign)
- Chancellor
- Vice Chancellor for Academic Affairs
- Associate Vice Chancellor for Academic Affairs
- University Librarian

Organization of the Institution

In terms of day-to-day operations, the Urbana-Champaign and Chicago campuses function fairly independently of each other. The vice president for academic affairs at the system level is primarily responsible for coordinating and balancing needs and priorities of the two campuses, particularly with regard to the budgeting process (i.e., budget development and submission to the state legislature) and subsequent allocation of resources.

Most business functions are handled at the system level by central administration. Fiduciary responsibilities of accounting, capital budgeting, facilities planning, administrative data processing, and purchasing are all centrally controlled. Academic computing, however, is decentralized and falls under the Computing Services Office (CSO) at the Urbana campus; the CSO reports to the vice chancellor for research.

Each campus is managed by its respective chancellor, under whom there are four vice chancellors. The university librarian reports directly to the vice chancellor for academic affairs, as do all the deans. Meetings of the "deans' group" are held on a monthly basis to keep members informed of developments on campus and throughout the university.

Organization of the Library

The University of Illinois Library at Urbana-Champaign is largely decentralized, comprising 39 departmental libraries and special collections. Each departmental library has its own faculty library committee, which makes decisions on related priorities and issues. The current librarian, Hugh Atkinson, who has held that position for eight years (after serving in the same capacity at Ohio State University), is a strong proponent of a decentralized library system. With this approach, he has moved away from the traditional library management practice of progressively consolidating various units.

Atkinson sees several advantages to a decentralized library. First, by locating departmental libraries near those academic units that are the heaviest users of specific collections, it provides scholars more time for actual research. Furthermore, new technologies provide users at remote sites with information on availability of materials at other locations, thus saving time in finding materials. In the chancellor's opinion, "it is the best of both worlds." Although decentralization of library operations means that the university librarian relinquishes some direct control, this circumstance effectively builds strong support for the library because, according to university administrators at Urbana, it enables the library to respond better to user needs. Because each departmental library has its own faculty committee, in effect 10 percent of campus faculty are actively involved in library matters. The university librarian believes that encouraging active involvement of the academic community is a good way to generate needed support. When asked about a possible problem of coordination, he replied that this problem is preferable to that of lack of support.

Faculty Status of Librarians

Librarians at the University of Illinois have faculty status. The university librarian, who believes strongly that library priorities should be *user-driven*, considers his faculty status to be an asset in keeping library priorities congruent with faculty priorities. In his view, having faculty status produces a much better attitude among professional library staff.

The university librarian has also extended decentralization to the organization of library staff and the definition of their responsibilities. He believes strongly in the "holistic librarian," who has both the skills and the responsibility for performing all of the library's major functions—reference, acquisition, and cataloging—within a given subject. He has, for example, bridged the traditional dichotomy between public and technical services by dissolving the cataloging department and moving its professional cataloging staff into public service units. Catalogers now are learning to do reference work, and reference librarians are learning how to catalog. However, a centralized cataloging unit remains, which primarily searches national databases for cataloging that already has been done elsewhere. Only those books for which copy cannot be found in the database are sent on to professional catalogers in the public service units.

Institutional Planning

Decentralized management combined with group planning and policy making is the norm at the University of Illinois. The two campuses have sufficient autonomy and flexibility to manage their respective operations with minimal intervention from the system level. Priorities, as reflected in the budgets, are generally campus-generated. There is budgetary flexibility once allocation decisions have been made by the state legislature and later by central administration. Academic units also have a degree of management autonomy and budgetary flexibility and decide on respective priorities during initial stages of the budgetary process.

The major policy-making body for the university system is the policy council, composed of the following nine members: the president, two vice presidents (for academic affairs and for business and finance), two chancellors, executive assistant to the president, director of public affairs, university legal counsel, and secretary to the board of trustees. The policy council meets twice a month, once prior to the regular meeting of the board of trustees, to discuss issues of significance to the university.

Another universitywide management group is the planning council, which is one level below the policy council. The planning council is chaired by the vice president for academic affairs and includes the vice president for business and finance, the four vice chancellors of the Urbana campus, the four vice chancellors of the Chicago campus, and four faculty representatives. The planning council advises the president, who brings recommendations from this group to the attention of the policy council, which makes final decisions. The planning council is the mechanism through which the university budget is generated.

On the UI-UC campus there is a chancellor's cabinet, which consists of the four vice chancellors and other key staff, such as the associate vice chancellor for public affairs. The cabinet has a maximum of 12 members and meets irregularly every one or two weeks.

The faculty senate is another important campus group. Traditionally, it has focused on budgetary issues. Recently, however, the senate at Urbana-Champaign has become increasingly concerned with interrelationships between campuses and with operations of the university system.

Planning for a given campus is mainly the chancellor's responsibility. At Urbana-Champaign, the chancellor delegates authority for academic planning and budgeting to the vice chancellor for academic affairs. In

1984, UI-UC developed a five-year plan. For this, the deans and university librarian were asked to submit five-year plans to the academic vice chancellor, who in turn developed a five-year plan for the campus.

Formal long-term planning has not been a tradition at the University of Illinois. Senior administrators have expressed some skepticism about the usefulness of long-range planning, which is viewed as somewhat limiting to the institution, and as a process that is more applicable to developing institutions than to one like Illinois, which is well-established. However, the president thinks that a long-range plan enables better support for budgetary positions. The plan is also a priority of the new chancellor at Urbana-Champaign because, in his view, it embodies the university's future aspirations and serves as an effective fund-raising tool.

Planning for the Library

The university librarian obtains advice on matters pertaining to overall library management from four groups: the executive committee, the administrative committee, the faculty senate library committee, and department heads.
  1. *Executive Committee.* Established by statute, this committee comprises eight members who are nominated and elected by the faculty for a two-year term. The group functions mainly as adviser to the university librarian on a variety of academic and administrative issues related to the library. It meets once every three weeks.
  2. *Administrative Committee.* This group is comprised of all library directors and assistant directors and meets every three weeks.
  3. *Faculty Senate Library Committee.* This committee meets monthly to advise the university librarian on the materials budget, allocation of book funds, and other issues that are brought to its attention.
  4. *Department Heads.* The university librarian meets daily with the director of general library services, the director of departmental library services, and the director of library collections. This group is enlarged two times a week to include the director of administrative services, the director of development, and the personnel manager. Department heads of General Services and Departmental Library Services meet with their own directors.

The university librarian also obtains suggestions from faculty committees of departmental libraries.

As mentioned previously concerning the campus level, the university librarian and deans of 15 major academic units meet monthly with the vice chancellor for academic affairs. The university librarian considers this meeting very important, because he believes campus policies are not formally developed but rather evolve through informal discussions of the group. At these meetings, Atkinson is "a partner with the deans in an educational enterprise." As such, it is important for him to keep in touch regularly with campus administrators, to keep them informed of library developments, and also to keep himself informed about developments in other campus units.

Budgeting Process

Each fall, heads of the various academic units, including the university librarian, submit a brief statement of budgetary needs to the academic vice chancellor, who then reviews the various requests with two groups: (1) a small group of academic administrators and (2) the faculty advisory committee on campus priorities. The academic vice chancellor then makes budget recommendations to the chancellor's advisory committee on the budget, after which a final decision is made by the chancellor and the academic vice chancellor. When the budget is approved by the state legislature, the academic vice chancellor makes budget allocations to academic units, and unit heads have the autonomy to allocate funds later within their own departments. UI-UC has an incremental budgeting system, with justification necessary only for increases over the previous year and for new programs.

The advisory committee on campus priorities is a fifteen-member group comprising eleven faculty, two students, and two professional administrators. The incumbent vice chancellor established this committee during a period of budget reductions. The associate vice chancellor for academic affairs is executive secretary to the committee, and is responsible for monitoring the operating budgets of the various units, providing back-up information, and recommending unit allocations to the academic vice chancellor. The chancellor's advisory committee on the budget comprises the four vice chancellors, two members of the faculty senate, and staff from the offices of the academic vice chancellor and chancellor.

Once a budget has been prepared by each campus, the university planning council, chaired by the vice president for academic affairs, formulates an integrated budget for the system in accordance with general legislative guidelines, for presentation to the state legislature. The academic vice president tries to balance the needs and priorities of the two campuses and coordinates their respective operating and capital budgets. He has powers of "persuasion and purse strings," and makes allocations to each campus.

Although in general the two campuses generate their own budget priorities, campus administrators often are invited to attend budget sessions, so that the campuses are aware of priorities of the state legislature and the governor. For example, in FY 1984 the state legislature placed a high priority on a back-to-basics program, which was not a campus priority in the initial budget formulation. The academic vice president provides campus administrators with information on legislative initiatives and other state priorities.

A single integrated budget for the entire university is submitted by the board of trustees to the State Board of Higher Education, which then makes budget recommendations to the General Assembly. The institutional budget also is submitted to the Bureau of Budget in the Governor's Office.

Factors considered in reviewing the library component of the university's budget request include inflation, usage statistics, purchasing patterns, and library performance in relation to peers (number of volumes held and expenditures per volume held).

Implementation and Control (Institutional Flexibility)

For various reasons, the university has considerable budgetary flexibility. Since the state legislature makes one appropriation to the university system, central administration has the flexibility to make campus allocations by object of expenditure (11 in all) in accordance with university priorities. The university also can move up to 2 percent of the total state appropriation between objects of expenditure, without the governor's approval. In addition, it is relatively easy to obtain approval to move funds exceeding this 2 percent limit.

Indirect cost recoveries (ICRs) are another avenue for budgetary flexibility. According to the associate vice chancellor for academic affairs, the rule of thumb is for 30 percent of ICRs to go to the college that received the grant and for 70 percent to go to the campus administration.

The University of Illinois currently enjoys strong support from the state legislature and governor. Higher education is a top priority of the governor, and there is generally full cooperation between the state legislature and institutions of higher education.

Implementation and Control (Library Flexibility)

Within the university, the library enjoys a degree of support similar to that given to UI by the state. Its budget base has been fairly stable. There were no budget reductions despite three to four years of university budget cuts. The academic vice chancellor at Urbana explained the situation as follows: "The library is a unit to which I can allocate money without being too concerned about balance across campus, since it serves everyone." Surplus funds at the end of the year are often allocated to the library by the academic vice chancellor. Of late, "bells have been ringing for the library," according to the vice president for business and finance, as demonstrated by the addition of stack No. 6 to library facilities.

Following the norm in the UI system, the university librarian can exercise some budgetary flexibility. For example, lapsed salaries and funds from the supplies budget were used to pay for additional terminals that were needed for the full bibliographic record (FBR) arrangement with the River Bend library system. The FBR arrangement required loading bibliographic information on 150,000 titles in the River Bend system's libraries into the UI system to demonstrate how a statewide system works.

Despite traditionally sufficient budgetary support and the university librarian's flexibility to manage the library, the latter incurred a budget deficit of $200,000 in FY 1984 and an additional $300,000 in FY 1985. The deficit was caused mainly by escalating costs of supplies and equipment (telephone and photocopying), operations and maintenance charges (maintenance of computers and other office equipment), and the cost of repairs to an aging physical plant.

Problems associated with an aging physical plant and facilities are not unique to the library. The vice president for academic affairs indicated that this is a universitywide problem that needs immediate attention. However, the library's problem is compounded by costs of new technologies that are needed to transform it from a labor-intensive to a more machine-intensive system.

At the campus level, budget deficits traditionally have been covered by using the university's contingency reserves or by reallocating funds. In the past, the academic vice chancellor has reallocated funds from one program area to another. However, campus administrators do not view these as an optimal approach to budget planning.

Two other problems related to the library budget are acquisitions and inadequate staffing levels. The acquisitions budget has lagged behind inflation for the last ten years. To correct this, a 15-percent increase is needed in the acquisitions budget for FY 1986. As for staffing levels needed to maintain current library services, there now is a shortage of ten professionals and ten to twenty clerical staff. The shortage could very well increase, depending on how library services are reorganized or otherwise changed in the future.

While being innovative and entrepreneurial in bringing the most current information technology to the library, Atkinson thinks it critical to keep library priorities congruent with overall university priorities. When asked how the library would respond to a 5-10 percent budget reduction or a similar increase, he said that it would depend on overall priorities. "The most obvious programmatic directions of the library will be defined by changes in the university program itself. Which disciplines are to be emphasized, which will be combined with other programs, and which will be separated will be a campus decision."

One of the chancellor's priorities is for UI-UC to fulfill its mission of service to the state. He perceives a need for "a better articulation in terms of our relationship to society." Hugh Atkinson's emphasis on statewide cooperation, including a plan to pursue cooperative collection development in the future, reflects a congruence of library and campus priorities.

Statewide Cooperative Efforts Among Libraries. In a state known for statewide cooperation among libraries, UI is a leader. In addition to being one of four members of ILLINET, the cooperative lending network, UI is involved with the Library Computer System (LCS), which is discussed more fully in the technology section.

Developing good will with other libraries in Illinois is part of the librarian's approach to building more support. He believes, for example, that cooperative efforts help strengthen the library's political base. Stack additions were a major priority of the university, but were No. 42 on the governor's priority list. By building up support among groups of public libraries and through discussions with state legislators, the library stack additions were moved to third place on the governor's priority list.

RESPONDING TO TECHNOLOGICAL CHANGE

The University of Illinois library is one of the most technologically advanced in the nation. Most basic functions—such as book acquisitions, serials check-in, and circulation—are automated. The card catalog also is automated, as is the interlibrary loan system within the state.

Library Computer System and Full Bibliographic Record (LCS and FBR)

In April 1985, the online catalog retrieval system, which supplants more than 12 million cards, was officially inaugurated. The university's online catalog is a pioneer in automating library services, as it is one of the first to serve as primary access to a large academic library (cards are no longer filed in the card catalog), the first to offer circulation information to most of the academic libraries (26 in all) in an entire state, and is an early system designed for users with no previous computer training.

The information system has two main components, the library computer system (LCS) and the full bibliographic record (FBR). LCS provides author and title location and availability of nearly all the University of Illinois library's 7 million volumes and of the volumes in 25 other academic libraries in the state. LCS links 26 academic libraries throughout Illinois by means of an online catalog retrieval system that provides information on nearly all UI-UC's volumes and those of the other 25 participating institutions. Members of LCS agree to extend the same borrowing privileges to faculty and students at other institutions that they provide to their own constituents.

LCS members pay only the costs of communication; not transaction costs to obtain the material. The University of Illinois is by far the heaviest interlibrary borrower among academic libraries in the country (126,329 transactions in FY 1985; the next heaviest borrowing was 17,413 transactions) and is one of two heaviest lenders. The university librarian estimates that UI-UC is unable to fulfill user needs only one-third of the time. The university librarian would like to reduce further this failure rate, partly by borrowing from other libraries, and has set a goal of increasing UI-UC's interlibrary borrowing to 200,000 annual transactions over a five-year period. That UI-UC is a net borrower goes against the conventional notion of large university libraries being net lenders. The university librarian explains it this way: ILLINET and LCS have gone beyond traditional interlibrary loans to become an extension of inhouse circulation.

FBR, the result of a joint project with the River Bend library system, Coal City, provides detailed information in a card catalog for 800,000 titles acquired by the University of Illinois library since 1975 and for 150,000 titles in the River Bend system's libraries. Both LCS and FBR systems are accessed through the same network of 250 terminals linked to a large computer in Chicago. The university librarian views the online system as "a prototype of a statewide catalog that adds to the description of books, information on their availability. It is designed so that many institutions can use it at once, it is economical, and it could serve the entire state." His goal is to eventually link together all libraries in the state so that they can use the catalog.

To provide physical access to materials from other libraries linked through LCS, there is also a statewide Interlibrary Delivery System

(ILDS). In the case of interlibrary loans, 80 percent of the time a book is placed on a loading dock within 24 hours and is mailed within two days. Also, an especially user-friendly computer program has been developed for the LCS system, to help University of Illinois students and faculty members locate books and periodicals in the 26 academic libraries. Linked to the electronically recorded library card catalog and circulation information, the program answers questions, offers instructions, and suggests ways to find titles or works on particular topics. Eleven personal computers in the main library and 47 more in 37 departmental libraries are controlled by a program developed by a UI-UC linguistics professor, and are linked to a mainframe in Chicago. According to program developer Professor Chang, "the fact that the interface is in a microcomputer points to the possibility of giving microcomputers a larger role in providing access to information retrieval systems."

Funding for the statewide LCS does not come from the library budget. However, at the system level, the office of the vice president for budget and finance provides support for certain business functions (equipment, trucks, and use of mainframe) and support for the administrative network (i.e., UI representatives to the LCS system).

LCS and FBR run on one of two IBM 3081s used for administrative computing. The UI-UC administrative computing center is located in Chicago, as are academic and administrative computing for the Chicago campus. Academic computing for Urbana-Champaign is handled by the Computing Services Office (CSO) on campus.

There are seven dial access ports to LCS. Two to three ports in the academic computing mainframes at each campus also provide LCS access. LCS is very efficient in terms of processing time and the load it places on the mainframe. There are 615 active terminals on the system, but current configuration allows for up to 800 terminals. Response time is virtually instantaneous.

An LCS policy council meets monthly to discuss system-related issues. The council consists of eight members, six of whom are directors of LCS libraries. One of the two University of Illinois librarians is always a member. Four members represent large libraries and two represent smaller libraries. The UI associate vice president for planning and budgeting serves as the institution's representative to the council and the vice president for university administrative information systems and services is the senior data processing representative. There is also an operations committee, composed of representatives from each of the 26 member libraries, which meets bimonthly. Both the LCS policy council and the operations committee are part of the Illinois Library

Computer Systems Organization. In addition, the user community is becoming increasingly involved in developing policies related to LCS.

The source of records for LCS is OCLC tapes. (UI-Urbana is the single largest contributor to the national OCLC cataloging data base.) Needed data for LCS is stripped from OCLC tapes. The UI-UC cataloging on OCLC is also the source for FBR records, which are loaded in Chicago by tape load, rather than directly through a printer port or on a record-by-record basis. A record exists in LCS for every book in the system, except for some materials in languages using nonroman characters.

FBR includes only titles that were cataloged through OCLC; for subject access to materials cataloged prior to OCLC, one must use the card catalog. Card filing, however, was stopped a few years ago, and patrons must use FBR for newer materials. Acquisitions and serials check-in are on LCS, which provides access to order records.

User Fees. While searches of LCS and FBR are free to the user, the library charges fees to recover most of the costs of an online bibliographic searching of commercial data bases such as those provided by Dialog and BRS. The cost currently ranges from $8-$12, and the library picks up only 10 percent of the cost. The university librarian would like to lower the charge, and eventually to provide the service for free. In principle, he is against user fees because he believes they run counter to the library's tradition.

Future Uses of Technology in the Library

LCS is scheduled to continue expanding its membership. To date, all requests to be included in the system have been accommodated. In addition, there currently is a proposal to include public libraries in the LCS system. Public libraries currently have reference access to the system. There are no immediate plans to expand FBR.

In terms of anticipated modifications, consideration is being given to purchasing software with more functions to link up with LCS. Eventually, LCS members may be able to buy their own acquisitions and serials check-in systems, as long as the systems can provide LCS with certain types of data.

New technologies play a prominent part in future plans for the library. In the university librarian's view the most important change in the library's role will be to provide machine-readable, nonbibliographic data.

While an actual blueprint has not been developed, it is certain that:

The library will have to store, index, and translate into a standard format or a series of standard formats a large mass of both locally compiled data and commercially available data as well. The problems are enormous and the expense of such collection will not be inconsiderable. The library will have to make provisions for at least a yearly refreshing of the data if it is stored in magnetic format and to provide both the programs for manipulation and analysis as well as the data itself. Indexes of variables and facilities for pilot programs will have to be available. An environment which is friendly to such data and machines to use it will have to be provided as well as work space and reference assistance. Housekeeping chores will have to be done. It also will put demands on space and other resources.

The second major change that the university librarian expects will be the rise of electronic journals and reference books. Atkinson foresees this change occurring in the next decade, and states that the electronic transmission of data will change radically the manner in which faculty and students use library services. He noted that:

> The rise of the machine-readable catalog, the automated circulation systems, the statewide sharing programs, and the electronic journals may well require a different set of hours of service at least for the electronic portion of the library's services and materials. The almost universal ownership of personal computers or TV set terminals may require that the library operates at least some services on a twenty-four-hour-a-day basis. Patron demands may require such a change.

University Plans for Technological Change

The university itself has plans for implementing new information systems and technologies. These plans center around the development and implementation of a Local Area Network (LAN). Current plans call for rewiring the system so that LANs are placed on each campus first and that by 1986 both campuses are linked through fiber optic cables. The LAN will incorporate voice, video, data, and telephone components. Supercomputers were scheduled to be in use by late 1985.

The associate vice president for administrative information systems and services, who reports to the vice president for business and finance, is responsible for developing the LAN's architecture. He is also a university representative to the LCS policy council.

The vice president for business and finance, who was instrumental in determining telecommunications needs, sees escalating costs of communications as the driving force in the development of LANs. The library has little involvement in such development; Hugh Atkinson is "relying on good systems people" to develop the LANs and to incorporate library operations appropriately.

The improvement of current information systems and the implementation of new information technologies are high on UI-UC Chancellor Everhart's priority list. Promoting computer literacy among faculty members and developing relationships with corporations are two activities that he would like to pursue, and the university is already starting to move in these directions. For example, the online retrieval system at the library, with access to LCS and FBR, is an excellent tool for developing computer literacy among faculty and students alike. Also in recent years, the university has received a number of grants for technological advancements, including a $12-million grant from IBM, larger grants from AT&T and Texas Instruments, and a $75- million grant from the National Science Foundation for a supercomputer.

SUMMARY

The University of Illinois library is one of the most successful in responding to technological change. Automation of most of its basic functions, implementation of LCS and FBR, and its various statewide cooperative arrangements with other libraries involve new information technologies and provide users a wider array of services more effectively than was done previously.

Various factors account for the library's effectiveness. First is the support that it traditionally has received from the university, which has been committed to maintaining the UI library's reputation. Faculty and administration involvement in planning also has contributed to the success of the library as well as of the institution. Higher education is a high priority in the state, and this is reflected in strong support for statewide cooperative efforts involving academic and public libraries.

In addition to support from both the university and the state legislature, the library has benefited from the proactive approach of the university librarian. He has been an innovator in transforming the library from its traditional role as a book repository and lender to that of purveyor of a wide array of information to a variety of users. He has sought additional sources of support through development efforts and statewide arrangements. In addition, he has tried to reinforce university priorities. For example, he has tried to be responsive to the needs of users not only in the university but throughout the state, through the implementation of new technologies and through active involvement in statewide library networks. He has developed support from constituents in several ways, one of which was to engender stronger faculty support through creation of faculty committees for each departmental library in a decentralized system.

Future plans emphasize advancement of the library in the field of information technology, for example, through the provision of machine-readable, nonbibliographic data. Because of strong state and university support and the university librarian's ability to maintain this support through technological innovations that are responsive to user needs, the UI library has a high probability of retaining its position as one of the most technologically innovative libraries in the country.

NEW YORK UNIVERSITY

"What should be clear to us by this time is that libraries cannot afford to hold out . . . or we might very well be frozen out. Technology will play an ever-increasing role in information exchange. If we want a future that is anything like our past, then we must begin to move towards automation."
   Carlton Rochell, Dean of the Libraries
   New York University

BACKGROUND

Institutional Profile

Located in a major urban and cultural center, New York University (NYU) is the largest private university in the United States. Headcount enrollment as of fall 1983 totalled 46,369. Enrollments were largest in graduate and professional programs—18,417. Approximately 14,800 students were enrolled in undergraduate programs and 13,140 in non-credit programs. Of a total 7,642 degrees conferred in 1983-84, the greatest number were master's degrees (3,747), followed by baccalaureate (2,541), professional (698), doctorate (425), and associate (231). Serving this student body were 13,100 employees, of which 4,700 were faculty (2,500 full-time and 2,200 part-time), 1,700 professional and administrative staff, 6,400 clerical and technical employees, and 300 service and ancillary staff.

The university includes fourteen schools, colleges, and divisions, and occupies six major centers in Manhattan. It also operates branch campuses and research programs in other parts of the United States and abroad, as well as twelve study programs in eleven countries.

When founded in 1831, New York University was envisioned as a new kind of American university, one that would broaden the scope of instruction beyond the traditional classical curriculum to include "useful" subjects such as history, political economy, and natural science. Educational offerings were "to correspond with the spirit and wants of our age and country, which shall be commensurate with our great and growing population" (*New York University Annual Report, 1983-84*, p. 12). The broadly based curriculum with a liberal foundation was to be made more widely available, with the new university being planned as one "which shall enlarge the opportunities of education for such youth as shall be found qualified. . . ." (*NYU Annual Report*, p. 12).

That NYU's founding philosophy has continued to guide it over a period of more than 150 years is reflected in the fact that the university provides financial aid to nearly three-quarters of its students. More than 80 percent work at least part-time to help defray the cost of their education. At the undergraduate level, not only do programs address students' financial needs, but they also encourage excellence and creativity through a growing program of merit scholarships.

The liberal arts tradition remains strong: the Washington Square and University College of Arts and Sciences has implemented a rigorous core curriculum, the Liberal Education Program (LEP). Professional schools continue to attract qualified students and include: the Tisch

New York University

School of the Arts, with outstanding programs in film, television, and the performing arts; the Courant Institute of Mathematical Sciences with its world-renowned computer science and applied mathematics programs; the Institute of Fine Arts; and the Graduate School of Business Administration, whose faculty and academic programs are regularly ranked among the top ten in the nation.

Although NYU has adhered to its traditional educational philosophy, the university today is very different from what it was. Responding to changing student needs has increased both the size and diversity of the university, to the extent that it now faces a major transition from having a primarily commuter student body to having one that is increasingly residential. The university also is involved in cooperative arrangements with other institutions in New York City to provide more opportunities to students. For example, it offers a combined Bachelor of Arts-Bachelor of Engineering degree program with nearby Cooper Union, as well as cooperative programs in art history and museum management in conjunction with the Metropolitan Museum of Art.

Library Profile

New York University Libraries, with 2,815,357 volumes as of FY 1984, is the twenty-fifth largest academic library in the country. NYU has seven libraries, but only Bobst (the main library), the library of the Institute of Fine Arts, and the library of the Graduate School of Business Administration report to Carlton Rochell, the dean of libraries. Libraries of the law, dental, and medical schools and that of the Courant Institute report to their respective deans. Staff for all seven libraries totals 343, including student workers. There are 97 professional staff and 178 support staff. Total library expenditures in FY 1984 were $10,035,266, or 2.5 percent of NYU's educational and general expenditures, which were $404,824,000. A total of $3,060,203 (30.5 percent) was spent on books, periodicals, and other research materials (*ARL Statistics, 1983-84*. Washington, D.C.: Association of Research Libraries, 1985).

Bobst library (the main library and the focus of this case study) is the largest physical structure at NYU. Often it is viewed as the center of the Washington Square campus, partly because it is a striking building with a 12-story atrium at its center. Bookstacks and public service centers wrap around three sides of the atrium. The library is featured often in NYU's annual reports and is the scene of major fund-raising activities and other university events. Extensive study facilities remain open until early morning, thus making the library a main study area on campus. Another important reason why Bobst is perceived as the center of campus is that offices of the university administration, including that of the president, are housed in the two top floors. At present, Bobst houses not only library facilities, but also those of the NYU Press and university archives.

Built a little more than ten years ago, Bobst is a relatively new library. The concept of having a central library at NYU is itself new, dating from the time when Bobst was built. On its completion, 30 separate library collections and staffs were transferred to the new building and library holdings were merged into one main collection. Merging the separate collections was a major task for the current dean of libraries when he assumed the position in 1976. Prior to his tenure at NYU, the current dean of libraries was director of the Atlanta Public Library.

Several collections of Bobst library are particularly notable. An example is the most comprehensive collection of United Nations documents and publications outside the U.N. itself. Further, the Tamiment library holds research vital to studying the American labor movement, and the Robert F. Wagner Labor Archives, located within the Tamiment library, is an invaluable collection of materials on the history and growth of trade unions in New York City. The Fales library holds a significant collection of nineteenth- and twentieth-century English and American literature and the Jerome S. Coles science library contains a unique collection of Russian scientific journals in translation.

Sources of Revenue and Levels of Expenditure

The Institution. Exhibit I shows New York University's revenues and expenditures for fiscal years 1983 and 1984. Revenues from the university's medical center accounted for approximately 50 percent of NYU's operating budget of about $650 million for FY 1984. Hospital revenues are the largest single item in this category. If only nonhospital revenues are considered, tuition and fees, including auxiliary fees, would account for 71 percent of NYU's Washington Square current unrestricted revenues. As with many independent universities, only a small portion of NYU's operating budget comes from state funds, and government grants and contracts mostly support its research activities.

Fund raising, a long-time university activity, has become more important in the last three years. Major fund raising started in fall 1982, when NYU embarked on "the most ambitious fund-raising campaign in its history—a two-year drive for $100 million—$1 million a week for 100 weeks" (*NYU Annual Report*, p.1). The university surpassed this goal, raising $110 million between September 1982 and August

EXHIBIT I

New York University
Statement of Current Funds Revenues, Expenditures, and Transfers

For the years ended August 31, 1984 and 1983

In thousands of dollars

	1984			1983
	Unrestricted	Restricted	Total	
Revenues:				
Tuition and fees	$198,024		$198,024	$181,650
Governmental appropriations	15,426		15,426	16,252
Gifts, grants, and contracts	12,795	$103,464	116,259	104,674
Endowment income	26,268	4,856	31,124	29,404
Hospitals and clinics	180,731		180,731	168,864
Indirect cost recovery on research and sponsored programs	22,138		22,138	19,570
Auxiliary enterprises	24,830		24,830	21,779
Real estate properties	13,883		13,883	13,089
Other	28,595	19,862	48,457	40,893
Total revenues	$522,690	$128,182	$650,872	$596,175
Expenditures and Transfers:				
Instruction and other academic programs	$156,292	$ 31,636	$187,928	$172,722
Patient-care services	138,800	3,119	141,919	130,286
Research and other sponsored programs		87,924	87,924	85,587
Libraries	9,575	1,169	10,744	9,650
Student services	12,769		12,769	11,501
Student aid	21,139	4,334	25,473	20,835
Operation of plant	51,349		51,349	46,157
Institutional services	33,898		33,898	30,811
General expenses	15,480		15,480	12,350
Mandatory transfers for:				
Debt service	12,811		12,811	11,846
Depreciation of hospital units' fixed assets	7,676		7,676	5,515
Student loan fund matching grants	210		210	244
Total educational and general	459,999	128,182	588,181	537,504
Auxiliary enterprises:				
Operating costs	21,083		21,083	18,791
Mandatory transfers for debt service	2,735		2,735	2,748
Real estate properties:				
Operating costs	10,478		10,478	9,714

EXHIBIT I (continued)

New York University
Statement of Current Funds Revenues, Expenditures, and Transfers

Mandatory transfers for debt service...	2,754		2,754	2,700
Total expenditures and mandatory transfers..............	497,049	128,182	625,231	571,457
Appropriations to (from) other funds—net:				
Plant funds for capital improvements, etc.......................	10,786		10,786	10,012
Quasi-endowment:				
Reinvested endowment income...	8,476		8,476	8,809
Other..	4,310		4,310	2,958
Other funds......................................	279		279	1,629
Net addition to current unrestricted fund balance—designated	1,790		1,790	1,310
Total expenditures and net transfers................................	$522,690	$128,182	$650,872	$596,175

1984. Over a nine-year period (1975-1984), yearly fund raising increased by 154 percent.

As for donors by constituency for the $100-million campaign, foundations accounted for 27.6 percent; nonalumni, 24.8 percent; trustees, 18.4 percent; corporations, 13.6 percent; alumni, 9.8 percent; and other groups, 5.8 percent. Foundations are significant not only for having contributed the highest percentage of donations, but also because in 1982-83, New York University was ranked third among colleges and universities that received foundation support, topped only by Harvard and Stanford (*Who Gets the Most from Foundations*, published by the Council for Financial Aid to Education).

The priority for revenues received from the two-year campaign was not bricks and mortar, but continued pursuit of academic excellence through increased support for both junior and senior faculty, scholarship aid, and program and research development. One high-priority area was arts and sciences. The campaign's success not only strengthened both program development and scholarship aid in this area, but permitted six endowed professorships to be established.

Despite successful development efforts, it is felt that the university is still underendowed, with an endowment of about $384 million to support 46,000 students. President Brademas strongly recommended in

1984 that the university establish a goal of raising $1 billion over a fifteen-year period, by the year 2000. The university administration encourages the different schools, through their deans, to raise external funds on their own. In this regard, NYU's location in New York City, a major financial center and home to several large corporations and foundations, is a major asset.

The Library. Sources of funds for FY 1983-84 for the Division of Libraries (including Bobst, Institute of Fine Arts, and the graduate business school) are the university, endowments, and restricted accounts. Actual endowment funds are about $2.8 million. These restricted accounts can be used for more general purposes than endowment funds. This category of funds includes revolving accounts, such as that for the Research Library Association of South Manhattan, a consortium established by NYU which includes Parsons School of Design, the New School for Social Research, and Cooper Union for the Advancement of Science and Art. This consortium is described in a later section.

Fund raising has become more important for the Bobst library as it has for NYU as a whole. The library's endowment growth pattern over a five-year period is shown below:

August 1980	$1.403 million
1981	1.538 million
1982	1.711 million
1983	1.893 million
1984	2.534 million

The sizable increase from 1983 to 1984 was due mainly to the establishment of the Mamdouha Bobst Book Endowment Fund, through a gift of $500,000 from the Elmer and Mamdouha Bobst Foundation. Events related to the tenth-anniversary celebration of Bobst also helped. Additional contributions from Mrs. Bobst and friends of the library made possible the establishment of Bobst Awards in Arts and Letters, given recently to eminent critics and writers such as Malcolm Cowley and Eudora Welty.

In spring 1984, the current dean initiated the establishment of the Friends of Bobst Library to support library collections and services. Chartered membership invitations were sent to past and prospective library supporters and to persons who had registered in the library's access office. Within a short time, the Friends enlisted 55 members and raised $11,170.

As stated in the 1983-84 annual report by the dean of libraries, "the importance of the library's fund-raising program cannot be overestimated when reviewing the fiscal capacity of the organization to meet current and future informational needs of the university" (*Library Annual Report*, p. 58). To help raise external funds, the university development office recently established a full-time position for a development officer to work solely on library programs. This position is to be subsidized by the library and is to have responsibility for overseeing the Friends, the awards dinner and similar gala events, corporate donations, foundation relations, and external public affairs.

PLANNING AND MANAGEMENT PROCESSES

The following persons were interviewed at New York University:

Vice Chancellor
Treasurer
Deputy Vice President for Budget and Planning
Assistant Vice President for External Affairs
University Development Officer
Director of the University Computer Center
Director of Academic Computing
Dean of the Libraries
Director of Fiscal Affairs for the Library

Organization of the Institution

When asked to describe the administrative structure of NYU, one senior administrator said, "We are a federated institution, like most multi-universities." Management responsibilities are vested largely in the 17 academic deans, who are given wide latitude for planning and other management programs, including fund-raising efforts.

NYU is governed by a board of trustees. The president is chief executive officer and the chancellor is chief academic officer. The current president, Brademas, has chosen to focus on developing external relations and, as a consequence, has delegated to the chancellor much responsibility for the university's internal management. One senior administrator described the central administration as being "very lean, a small pyramid with a lot of interface between small groups."

All vice presidents and deans, including the dean of libraries, report to the chancellor. Weekly deans' meetings are chaired by the president. Because development activities are very important at NYU, the dean of libraries works with the vice president for external affairs and the president on fund-raising matters. This dual reporting relationship is a carry-over from arrangements worked out by the current dean with previous administrations.

As noted, academic deans have substantial management responsibilities. In the chancellor's absence, decisions on matters pertaining to the various schools are delegated to their deans.

In addition to the senior management structure, there is also a university senate, which consists of representatives from various campus constituencies, such as the faculty council, the student council, and the university administrative council. The senate finance committee included representatives from each of these four constituent groups. All members of the deans' council are members of the senate.

Organization of the Library

As indicated earlier, the concept of a main library is fairly new at NYU. The university used to have two campuses, Washington Square and University Heights. Prior to establishing the Bobst library in 1973, each campus had its own library dean and staff. Under the old organizational structure, there was no coordinated collection-development effort.

Even with the establishment of a main library, the NYU libraries are still somewhat decentralized. It will be recalled that the dean of libraries has jurisdiction over Bobst and two other libraries: those of the Graduate School of Business Administration and of the Institute of Fine Arts. Also, the other four libraries—serving the medical, dental, and law schools and the Courant Institute—report to the deans of their respective schools. This organizational arrangement can create problems in planning cohesive library programs, as discussed later.

Directors of the major administrative divisions—technical and automated services, collection management and consortial services, and public and administrative services—and the library fiscal officer form the libraries cabinet, which helps the dean with planning and policy decisions. Previously, there was a university senate, ad hoc library committee. However, the ad hoc committee was highly politicized, according to the current dean of libraries, and therefore was not as effective as it could have been in pursuing library interests. After the first year of the current dean's tenure, members of the ad hoc committee were not replaced. Currently, each faculty member works with subject specialists on matters relating to collection development.

Approximately two-thirds of the present library faculty were appointed by the current dean. Librarians at NYU have faculty status. Within the last few years, the library faculty council recommended that they be excluded from the tenure system, but the recommendation was vetoed by the university faculty council. The library faculty, however, succeeded in modifying the criteria for tenure, shifting the emphasis from publication to job performance.

The dean of libraries also has jurisdiction over university archives and the NYU Press. The libraries' relationship with the university computer center (used for administrative computing) is mostly informal, primarily through the current dean's direct involvement in the universitywide telecommunications committee, which plans the university's future direction in information technology.

Planning for the Institution

Planning at NYU has been mostly an informal process, undertaken primarily by the various schools. According to the vice chancellor, the schools always have been encouraged to use their own initiative in program planning and development efforts. Coordination takes place at the weekly deans' meeting, where, according to the vice chancellor, "both process and substance are discussed," and "deans gain a healthy respect for one another's priorities." The deans' council is described by one administrator as a management group, not an academic forum.

In 1984-85, a formal long-range planning process at NYU was instituted for the first time. As President Brademas expressed the need for it: "Great universities . . . , like business and government, must plan at least ten to fifteen years ahead" (*1983-84 Annual Report*, p. 19). There have been previous planning efforts, but these have concentrated on specific areas, such as the use of computers, and not on NYU as a whole. In 1984, the chancellor circulated a document that outlined the process of formulating a five-year plan for the university.

Development is another area for which there has been coordinated planning. While schools generate their own fund-raising priorities, NYU's central development office coordinates priorities and efforts, so that prospective donors are not subjected to several solicitations and so that the best match between donor and school can be achieved. The central office also supports schools in their efforts to solicit corporate giving. Development managers of the different schools meet once a month to discuss plans and activities, and they submit biweekly reports to the university development officer. The vice president for external affairs and the assistant vice president for external affairs meet every two weeks, and senior staff of the central development office meet weekly. These streamlined processes and procedures were implemented in the last three to four years.

The recently initiated, long-range planning process will continue to focus on the two key areas of technology and development. A telecommunications committee, composed of vice presidents and deans and including the dean of libraries, is planning implementation of local area networks (LANs) throughout the university. The Committee for the Year 2000, composed of trustees appointed by the president, has been assigned the task of assessing NYU's fund-raising needs and fund-raising potential over the next 15 years with the goal of raising $1 billion by the year 2000.

Planning for the Library

Planning for the library, as with planning at NYU in general, is informal. The dean of libraries established three separate structures to address different areas; the libraries cabinet, chaired by the dean and composed of directors of major administrative divisions, oversees day-to-day operations and considers overall management issues. The library's department and unit heads meet monthly with the dean to review administrative matters. The library faculty, which meets four times per year, considers faculty welfare issues, such as promotion and tenure, and academic perquisites. To facilitate efficient administration of the library, the dean tries to keep department agendas, department unit heads' meetings, and faculty meetings from overlapping.

Because formal long-range planning was instituted only recently at NYU, most planning efforts in the library have been related to the annual budgetary and annual report process. All deans are required to submit an annual planning report to the chancellor each November. This report sets the context for the next fiscal year's budget. In preparing the annual report and the budget report, deans use a staffing plan memorandum and budget guidelines that are issued to them about a month before reports are due. The dean of libraries asks library directors to state their needs and priorities and the directors in turn solicit information from units that report to them. During this annual review process, individual departmental goals are set and priorities are considered by the libraries cabinet and the library faculty budget advisory committee. Following a series of discussions and review sessions, major programmatic thrusts are decided on, such as the recent emphasis on stable funding for the Tamiment Institute library, which contains rich documentation on the history of American labor.

In their planning reports, deans are expected to give an overall evaluation of their respective school in terms of accomplishments and problems in the last year, ways in which the school's goals were met, and major challenges ahead. The evaluation also should indicate the school's academic strengths and weaknesses, as well as provide specific recommendations on staffing, enrollment, and budgetary issues. The NYU Libraries' priorities for 1984-85 included retrospective conversion, acquisitions, and better user-support services. For example, photocopying services improved when a contract with an outside vendor was terminated and services were provided in-house.

The dean of libraries has several opportunities to influence universitywide planning. The first is through the deans' council, the university senate and its committees, and the university graduate commission. The second is through the deans' involvement on a telecommunications committee, which is in charge of planning NYU's future in information technology. The third avenue of influence is in development, or fund-raising activities, which is a priority of the president and the board of trustees. The current dean has been active in fund-raising efforts to support both technological advances and collection development for the library. Partly because of these activities, he was able to secure a high-level development officer, who works exclusively on library affairs. The library development office is housed in the Bobst library and is supported partly by library funds, an arrangement that is atypical at NYU.

Budgeting for the Institution

Exhibit II shows the 1985-86 budget calendar of NYU's Washington Square campus. All deans, including the dean of libraries, submit an annual budget. The budget submission process is twofold: requests for operating and capital budgets are submitted to the deputy vice president for budget and planning; earlier, a staffing request is submitted to the vice chancellor.

As part of the "annual report" process, school deans answer a series of questions each summer regarding budget needs, fund raising, and special problems.

In October, deans receive a staffing plan memorandum and discuss their staffing needs in a series of meetings with the vice chancellor and chancellor, who chairs these meetings. The deputy vice president for budget and planning chairs budget meetings at which financial aspects are discussed. Budget and academic officers attend each meeting. Deans are given budgetary guidelines to which they can suggest changes and additional considerations. Inflation measures are, of course, part of budget guidelines. According to the deputy vice president for budget and planning, the administration is aware that certain library costs, particularly of materials, exceed national inflation guidelines.

To prepare for submission of a budget, each dean is given a spread-

New York University

EXHIBIT II

Washington Square 1985/86 Budget Calendar

Item	Due Date
1. Issuance of 1985/86 Staffing Plan Memorandum	October
2. Issuance of 1985/86 Budget Guidelines/Materials	November
3. Meetings on Planning Reports and Faculty Staffing Plans	November-January
4. Deans' and Vice Presidents' Fiscal Year 1986 Narrative and Revenue/Expense For Submission	January 11
5. Meetings to discuss Budget Plans with Deans, Vice Presidents, Senate Financial Affairs Committee, Deans' Council	January-February
6. Meetings with Trustee Budget Subcommittee to review Tuition/Salary Guidelines/University Financial Condition	January-February
7. Meeting with Trustee Executive Committee to review Tuition and Salary Guidelines	February 11
8. Board of Trustees Financial Affairs Committee Meeting to approve 1985/86 Tuition Rates/Auxiliary Rates/Compensation Policy	March 4
9. Full Board of Trustees Meeting to approve Tuition/Auxiliary Rates and Compensation Policy	March 11
10. Additional Discussions with Schools, Areas, Senate Finance Committee, and Trustee Subcommittees to finalize 1985/86 Revenue and Expense Budget	March-April
11. Formal Ratification of 1985/86 Budget by Board of Trustees	May 13
12. Submission by Schools and Areas of Salary Estimate Worksheets	May-June
13. Submission by Schools and Areas of Budget Estimate Worksheets	May-July
14. Formulation of University 1985/86 Base Budget	August
15. Start of 1985/86 Fiscal Year	September 1

sheet on the current fiscal year's budget. The deans are expected to justify how funds are currently spent or to make necessary modifications on budget worksheets provided for this purpose. They are, therefore, given the opportunity to recast their current revenue and expense budget to insure more accurate forecasts for the coming fiscal year. Requests for new funds for the current year that would require administrative approval cannot be shown as revisions to the current budget. Only after the current year's budget is justified or recast as needed can deans develop budget requests for the next year. Capital project proposals are submitted separately, ranked by priority.

The dean of libraries writes a detailed justification for every budget item, in order to communicate the library's financial needs clearly.

Although individual schools can indicate their priorities, they are requested to consider these priorities in the context of overall university needs. Current institutional priorities, according to the deputy vice president for budget and planning, are to maintain the following: stable enrollments, marketable tuition rates, sufficient student financial aid, and the excellence of the university's academic resources, of which the library is an important part. Another priority is to lobby for more federal and state funding, because there are limits to revenues that can be generated from tuition increases.

In their budget request, deans express their views on their general financial concerns, such as financial aid, deferred maintenance, library acquisitions, and computer enhancements. These issues and broad planning assumptions—such as projected tuition income, outlook on federal funds, other income projections, and implications of these factors for financial management of the university—are discussed at weekly meetings of the deans' council and in meetings with the president and chancellor. The dean of libraries describes the meetings as being conducted in an "advise and consent" mode.

School budget policy committees are usually consulted on school budget proposals. All budget requests are reviewed and approved by the chancellor, vice chancellor, senior vice president for finance, and deputy senior vice president for finance. The chancellor solicits advice from the university senate finance committee, which consists of representatives from the constituent groups of the university: deans, university administrators, faculty, and students. Specific budget decisions, such as approval of fund transfers, are made by the deputy vice president for budget and planning.

Budgeting for the Library

Within the library, line-item needs are developed by staff and presented to department heads. This is done in consultation with the library business officer, within the context of unit goals that are determined during an annual review process. Unit goals are used also by the libraries cabinet (the senior management group) to decide on programmatic directions for the coming year. The dean and library business officer consolidate requests from different units into a budget proposal, which is reviewed by the library faculty budget committee. (All schools are required to have a committee review as part of the budgetary process.) The chairperson of the library faculty budget committee reports on the budget proposal to the entire library faculty. Final decisions on budget proposals are made by the dean and cabinet.

Implementation and Control

A shared perception among university administrators is that NYU is doing well as an institution, but resources are definitely scarce. In the 1970s, the university suffered substantial financial losses, which resulted in eventual divestiture of the University Heights campus. The institution has since rebuilt its financial base, but there is a need to generate more resources to maintain and improve academic program offerings. A major constraint for NYU is that, if hospital revenues are excluded from the budget, institutional revenues are 71 percent tuition-fee driven. Federal funds for sponsored programs also are decreasing, which means that schools will have smaller amounts of indirect cost recoveries (ICRs), which they are allowed to retain.

To maintain its financial base, even "to survive," as one administrator put it, NYU uses several approaches. One that has already been discussed is aggressive fund raising. Development efforts, which previously were conducted centrally, are now coordinated by the office of the vice president for external affairs.

Like many other independent institutions in New York State, the university is lobbying for increased state funding. NYU is also highly leveraged. Debt financing has increased in the last few years to cover funding for additional university housing, which was needed because of an increase in the university's resident population.

Schools are further encouraged to operate independently by the administration's adherence to the philosophy of "every tub on its own bottom." At NYU, each unit covers all its direct costs plus a percentage of indirect costs. The library is, in fact, an important factor in what is described as a fairly detailed, cost-allocation system: all direct and indirect costs pertaining to library use are allocated to the various units on the basis of book circulation by school.

Deans are limited in their ability to transfer funds from one budget category to another. All such transfers must be approved by the deputy vice president for budget and planning. Furthermore, unexpended funds for nonpersonnel-related matters cannot be accrued, because these funds normally are reallocated to units that need extra resources.

Because of the scarcity of NYU's financial resources, internal control mechanisms are particularly important. One such mechanism, administered by the controller's office, is the Expenditure Control Report (ECR), which reflects the account structure of the approved budget. ECRs are generated on a monthly basis for each budgetary unit, indicating expenditures, encumbrances, and the unit's balance.

Library Flexibility. During the annual budget submission process, the library, like all the schools at NYU, competes for scarce university resources. The dean of libraries expressed the view that, historically speaking, the library has not been as well-funded as it should be. The materials budget, in particular, is inadequate, and increases are needed not only to match the rate of inflation in book and serial prices, but also to correct past deficiencies. Erratic funding in the past has meant that important serials were cancelled in certain years and buying was held to a minimal level. A major investment is needed to correct these deficiencies and to sustain the retrospective collecting that finally has begun.

In FY 1984-85, there were no automatic budget adjustments for inflation volume. However, in 1983-84 a total of $1,367,089 was available for the Bobst book and serial budgets, 10 percent more than in 1982-83. The collection development committee decided that both budgets should be increased 10 percent, allowing the library to maintain its present ratio of 45:55 for book and serial allocations. Within the book budget, the most generous increases were given to the humanities fund lines in anticipation of a year of active, retrospective collection building.

There is, however, some room for budgetary flexibility. The most obvious source of flexibility is the institution's entrepreneurial mode. The current dean of libraries initiated several fund-raising efforts that were successful enough to support the implementation of new technologies in the library, primarily the online catalog known as BOBCAT. The dean also implemented a consortial arrangement, the Research Library Association of South Manhattan, whereby three other institutions pay a fee to the NYU library in exchange for certain services, such as cataloging services, an automated circulation system, and dedicated telephone-line access to BOBCAT.

The dean's development efforts were given an added boost by the appointment of a full-time, high-level development officer for the library. Previously, the library had to share a development officer with a school. The library development officer is focusing efforts on three areas: (1) the Bobst literary awards, (2) funding for retrospective conversion of the card catalog, and (3) the Avery Fisher Center for Music and Media. The president and chancellor also support the library and its importance to the university. The president was already a strong proponent of libraries when he served in Congress.

The dean of libraries has some flexibility in using funds provided by the university. In summer, the library usually receives an additional $75,000-$100,000 from unexpended university funds. These additional funds are used for acquisitions and collection development. The university's location in New York City, which has many excellent libraries, including the New York public library, helps to focus collection development efforts. Because of this wealth of library resources in the city, it has been determined that the NYU library should concentrate on building a strong research collection, which would be of greater use to its faculty. Any increase or decrease in library funding, according to the dean, would have a corresponding effect on collection development. He indicated that, to the extent possible, library services will not be affected by decreases in funding.

The tradition of fostering independence among the schools has some disadvantages. In the case of the library, the dean of libraries' lack of jurisdiction over four of the seven NYU libraries has caused certain problems in coordinating plans for implementation of new technologies. The law library, for example, is in the process of developing its own online catalog, which, in view of the existence of BOBCAT, could mean duplication of costs and efforts.

The library's 1983-84 annual report highlighted the area of faculty and departmental liaison as one of concern. Faculty and graduate students in many departments do not know that the library has subject specialists in their areas. Many faculty members are inclined to think of librarians as conduits for book requests, rather than as specialists who should be consulted when new courses are being planned, or as colleagues to whom graduate students should be referred. For 1984-85, several steps were planned to encourage more open communication between the library and the various schools and their faculties. One step was to review each librarian's relations with his or her respective departments. Another was to add to the faculty information bulletin series a summary of various faculty services, including preferred methods for handling mass library assignments. Efforts already have been made to increase the involvement of faculty members in determining collection development policies. It is the dean's view that the gap between librarians and the teaching faculty must be narrowed if the library's potential for service is to be fully realized.

Evaluation

The Division of Libraries at NYU is perceived within the institution to be a technological leader. Its online catalog, BOBCAT, was successfully implemented under the current dean. As a result, library use has increased and library services have become more efficient. The library was among the first units on campus to implement a local area network (LAN). As a member of NYU's telecommunications committee, the dean of libraries is involved in universitywide plans for implementation of new information technologies, for example, the installation of a universitywide LAN.

In an institution that promotes independent fund-raising efforts, the dean of libraries is considered an entrepreneur, who has succeeded in obtaining external support to fund continued library improvements. BOBCAT development and implementation has been financed mostly by independent fund-raising efforts. The current dean also has been active in efforts to obtain a one-time state appropriation to strengthen the Robert F. Wagner Labor Archives collection, and make it a prestigious research facility for the history of labor in New York City.

RESPONDING TO TECHNOLOGICAL CHANGE

The major technological advancement of the library to date is BOBCAT, Bobst library's online catalog, inaugurated in September 1983. BOBCAT is a "search only" data resource from which information about holdings of NYU and three other libraries can be retrieved. BOBCAT represents one of the university's most important assets, since it has greatly enhanced access to library resources. By August 1984, 100 BOBCAT terminals were in operation, most of which were located on the 12 floors of the Bobst library. Terminals were provided to library staff in the departments of technical services, collection development, and interlibrary loan, and at each reference desk. In addition, terminals were placed in the Graduate School of Business Administration library, the Institute of Fine Arts library, the law school library, the New School, Parsons School of Design, and Cooper Union. By December 1984, each branch of the NYU library system and each member of the Research Library Association of South Manhattan had BOBCAT terminals connected to Bobst by leased telephone lines.

History of the System

What led to the development of BOBCAT? Perhaps the impetus can be traced to the creation in 1977 of the Research Library Association of South Manhattan, which was in large measure due to the efforts of the current dean of libraries, Carlton Rochell. The association was established as a resource-sharing consortium.

A combined catalog was an immediate priority of the consortium, with a choice between a computer-output microfilm (COM) system and an online system. The initial cost of the COM system was relatively low and it was simple and easily installed. However, it was not designed for users with complex research needs. Also, while it could hold a large database, the data could be manipulated only in limited ways. The COM system was also difficult to update.

The consortium, therefore, chose to have an online catalog because it provided more immediacy and flexibility, and was more cost-effective over the long term. Consultants were hired and initial studies explored organizational needs, technologies that could address these needs, and associated costs. Because there was no suitable existing system that could be adapted to NYU's user needs, it was decided that the library's online catalog would have to be developed.

A consultant was hired to develop system specifications, with emphasis on reliability and system performance. Other requirements were: (1) that the system be "user-friendly," one that would use existing library skills and was fairly self-instructional, and (2) that it be replicable, or such that other libraries could adapt it to their needs in areas such as circulation, reserve, and eventually, both acquisitions and serials check-in (this was a requirement of foundations that helped support the system's development).

Specifications also were drawn up for a system that would: (1) accept full MARC records from either OCLC or RLIN (Research Library Information Network); (2) display records in brief, full, or tagged form; and (3) offer users the option of saving citations in memory for later printout. The system had various access points—titles, subject, or key words. It also had various standard library numbers—Library of Congress card number, superintendent of documents number, and international standard numbers (ISBN and ISSN). It had a Boolean searching capability (the ability to broaden or narrow a search in a database by combining dissimilar terms using logical connectors such as "and," "or," and "not") and could restrict a search by language, format, or library location.

While system specifications were being developed, an automation committee was formed. There were 12 to 14 members, with representatives from each of the 4 members of the library consortium. The committee's role was not to contribute technical expertise to consultants, but to develop an awareness within the university about technological developments in library automation. The dean of libraries views this committee and its successor as being very valuable, because it insured the system's user-friendliness and kept both library patrons and staff aware of project developments.

After system specifications had been developed, the next major decision for the library was whether it should develop its own online catalog or purchase one from a vendor. NYU Libraries decided to use a vendor, the consensus being that there was "just too much time and too much money to be lost in an area where few libraries have much knowledge or experience" ("On the Road to LAN," NYU Library Report, p. 9). The decision also was made partly to resolve the problem of system integration. Since the library's plan was to link the online catalog to the circulation system, management thought it would be good to discuss catalog requirements with GEAC Canada Limited, a vendor with whom a circulation system was then being negotiated. Management eventually decided to use GEAC for both circulation and the online catalog systems. There were several reasons behind the choice of GEAC: (1) it had a reputation for system and hardware reliability; (2) it had considerable library experience, having been used by several libraries, mainly in Canada; (3) it was a well-capitalized firm; and (4) its representatives had good relations with the NYU library staff, a factor that, it was felt, would contribute to system and service reliability.

No written specifications were drawn up for the new circulation system because of severe time pressure, a result of the inadequacy of NYU's circulation system, which had become critical by 1980. This crisis had been precipitated by rapid deterioration of library circulation services, due to lack of needed technological capacity. As a consequence, the need for change was immediate. In this regard, a general requirement of a new circulation system was that it should possess all the capacities of the old system and more, and that the contract with the vendor have built-in performance criteria, with penalties for failure. The contract with GEAC included a maintenance agreement, RLIN interface, and specific acceptance tests for both equipment and system reliability.

NYU library was able to address the circulation problem quickly because university procurement procedures were less cumbersome than those of some public institutions. Once a vendor was chosen, for example, management could proceed immediately with contract negotiations. However, the current dean of libraries does not recommend such procurement procedures to other institutions unless a similar crisis should be involved. The process was different for the development of the online catalog, when GEAC had to tailor the system to specifications designed by NYU consultants.

Assessment of BOBCAT

As a first step toward determining necessary improvements in the system, the library embarked on a study of user reactions. Funding was provided by the Council on Library Resources and the Association of Research Libraries. To assess successful use of BOBCAT relative to stated levels of satisfaction, the library conducted 1,700 user surveys at various BOBCAT terminal sites during April and May 1984. Both users of BOBCAT and users of just the card catalog were selected to fill out a survey form.

BOBCAT has increased library use, as shown by a 30-percent increase in circulation after its installation. In one part of the study, 93 percent of the users expressed favorable views about BOBCAT. Seventy-eight percent stated they were satisfied with what they found in relation to what they sought. In terms of learning to use the catalog, 64 percent reported that they learned from instructions on the catalog screen, a dramatic difference from findings at 29 libraries with other online catalog systems. Among nonusers of BOBCAT, 35 percent reported that they felt it was easy to learn to use the online catalog, and 75 percent indicated they were likely to use it in the future. Among BOBCAT users, satisfaction paralleled success. Nearly 80 percent stated that they found all or some of the information they sought, and 75 percent indicated satisfaction with the search outcome.

Although user satisfaction with BOBCAT was evident from the survey, much remains to be done in order to realize the full benefits of the system. A major challenge, for example, will be the conversion of 600,000 bibliographic records now accessible only through the card catalog.

Retrospective Conversion

Because users have indicated a clear desire to have BOBCAT contain more records, the library has given high priority to converting as many card catalog records as possible to machine-readable form. Several retrospective conversion projects are planned and small grants have been received for this purpose. Funds made available through the Research Libraries Group (RLG) will allow creation of machine-readable records for certain monographic materials. Over the next two years, records for 11,000 music scores will be converted through RLIN, which also is being used for all current cataloging of music scores. A third RLG-funded project will convert 182 archival records, primarily from the University Archives and Wagner Labor Archives collections. Using a recently introduced format, this project will make records for a large number of archival materials available for the first time, through BOBCAT.

These projects, however, are a very small part of the retrospective conversion that is necessary to make all NYU collections accessible to BOBCAT users. To convert the approximately 600,000 monograph titles not in machine-readable form, a method available through Carrollton Press, Inc., has been selected that uses their MARC and REMARC databases. It is anticipated that the library staff, by using this method, will be able to key in all search requests over the next two years. This process is at least three times faster than it would be if the RLIN system were used and it requires no additional equipment. REMARC records from Carrollton will be loaded into BOBCAT on receipt. At the end of this process, between 75 and 80 percent of the monograph collection should be in machine-readable form and accessible through BOBCAT.

The conversion of serial holdings is a far more complex project. Some funding was expected in 1985, at which time the library staff were to begin converting records for currently received periodical titles. The pace of this project depends on available funding.

New System Developments

As staff of NYU work to improve BOBCAT, GEAC personnel and librarians at other universities are preparing additional online catalog enhancements. The Smithsonian Institution is helping GEAC test an authority-control system to insure consistent headings in the online catalog and permit universal changes of entries when necessary. In addition to staff at the Smithsonian, librarians from NYU and the University of Maryland also participated in designing the authority system. This shared approach to problem-solving draws on the expertise of many library staffs and makes catalog enhancements applicable to the systems of other institutions.

In addition to shared developments, GEAC is independently enhancing the BOBCAT system, such as by adding printing capability. This will allow users to save records in a small file, arrange them in preferred order (for example, by title), and then print them. Another GEAC project is the development of a back-up mechanism for use when the online catalog is not operating. This initially may take the form of a computer output microform catalog. For the long term, however, such advanced technology as the optical disk is being explored to provide a backup mechanism with the same access points as BOBCAT itself. All of these enhancements were to be made available to NYU users in 1985.

Future Plans

To expand BOBCAT's usefulness, circulation system data will be added to BOBCAT records, thus giving status information in response to a BOBCAT search. Respondents in the Online Catalog User Survey considered this improvement a priority.

Another step towards integrating the library's automated systems will be the addition of "on-order" and "in-process" records to BOBCAT. These will provide information on materials even before they have been cataloged.

BOBCAT is only the beginning of the library's conversion to a new mode of information delivery. It is just one of many information resources that will be available to scholars through local area networks (LANs), such as the one already installed at Bobst library. Dean Rochell envisions the following situation: using multifunctional terminals attached to LANs, scholars will be able to sit at their "workstations" and draw data from the local library catalog, manipulate it, search further for materials in other libraries throughout the world, then edit a document incorporating information gathered from the many files available through an extensive telecommunications network. Presently, library staff are beginning to experiment with multiple access capabilities to the online catalog, office automation system, and commercial databases provided to them through personal computers in conjunction with Bobst's LAN.

The local area network in Bobst now serves as a "data highway" for the library's circulation, catalog, and office automation functions. This relatively new computerized communications device operates on a coaxial cable running throughout the building and it can connect with the LAN that eventually will be in other buildings on campus. The LAN promotes resource sharing by allowing devices to use such common facilities as printers or computer ports and it permits them to communicate with any other device on the network. The LAN can easily accommodate 300 terminals operating at the same time, and as many as 1,000 devices can be connected without reducing response time.

Between 150 and 200 terminals soon will be using the LAN in Bobst. It is hoped that eventually Bobst's LAN will be linked with a universitywide LAN that will serve all of NYU's Washington Square campus. Thus, students and faculty using a terminal in their offices or dormitories will have access to the library's online catalog as well as to other computerized files available throughout the university.

This desired link with a universitywide LAN raises another issue. Where does NYU as an institution stand with regard to the implementation of new information technologies?

University Developments in Information Technology

In 1983, a data task force was formed to initiate plans and activities with regard to NYU's needs in information technology. The group was composed of both administrators and faculty, representing data communications suppliers and users from several areas within the university.

Following months of research and discussions, the task force developed a list of data requirements for inclusion in a request for proposal issued by the telecommunications office in March 1983 to replace the campus Centrex telephone system.

Subsequent technical analyses and meetings with vendors during mid- to late 1983 led the data task force to recommend that a LAN be implemented at the same time to address the university's nonvoice communications needs. The recommendation was based on the conclusion that the broadband alternative provided a cost-effective, stable technology currently used by a large number of universities and other organizations. In addition to comparatively low startup costs, the broadband LAN provided the "open system" environment and high capacity required by diverse university activities. Future applications such as security video, energy management, and mixed data/image activities, as well as extension of the LAN to new buildings and dormitories, could be accommodated by the broadband system with minimal impact on existing services.

Other benefits of a LAN are cost-effective support of a wide range of terminal, PC/workstation, and computer interconnection, which would facilitate sharing information and processing resources among members of the university community. It was felt that the use of a LAN as the primary nonvoice vehicle also would protect the new PBX from overload and premature operational obsolescence caused by large, unplanned data demands. In this regard the LAN would interface with the PBX and provide campuswide services for "casual" data users in locations where the broadband cable was not yet (or could not be) installed. The task force concluded that, given the anticipated growth rate for data connections and savings in LAN connections costs, a broadband LAN would pay back its startup costs within a one- to three-year period.

It is anticipated that the LAN will be installed in two phases. The first phase targets approximately 12 buildings with near-term, specific data requirements and the second phase is to address the remaining buildings at Washington Square. The first phase, currently being implemented, focuses on "pilot" applications so that users are given the opportunity to familiarize themselves with new technologies. On the scheduled universitywide implementation of the system in fall 1986, LAN data services will be available to users at approximately 87 percent of existing Washington Square telephone locations, as well as in classrooms and terminal cluster sites.

To insure successful implementation of the LAN at NYU, the data task force developed certain additional recommendations, of which the first and most immediate was to establish a permanent committee to discuss relevant issues and to coordinate program activities related to the network. Another recommendation was to start technical and budgetary planning for mainframe and terminal-user LAN connection equipment at major computer centers and user locations, to insure maximum compatibility and cost-effectiveness of equipment and services. Other recommendations pertained to technical requirements and alternatives for pathways and connections to remote campus locations (outside Washington Square), including the need to procure remote data carrier services.

The Library and Academic Computing

With regard to links with other computing units on campus, there are plans for more extensive interface between the library and the academic computing center. NYU long has had a computer center, which was often supported by contract funds. Originally, the computer center was part of the Courant Institute for Mathematical Sciences, and was used mainly to support the Institute's computing needs. In 1980, academic computing was introduced on campus and joined with Courant's computing efforts.

The academic computing center deals primarily with mainframes, whereas microcomputers are purchased and handled in a decentralized way. There is a cluster of microcomputers in the computer science department as well as in some other campus units. Clusters of terminals, including one in the library, also tie into the mainframe. From the perspective of the academic computing center, the following are possibilities for cooperative efforts between the library and academic computing:
1. The library can offer information on the availability of machine-readable data files (MRDFs) at the academic computing center.
2. BOBCAT lines can be made accessible to the academic community through a switch located in academic computing. This could provide a communications network until the LAN has been implemented throughout the institution.
3. The library can continue to function and even perhaps expand as a location for terminals. Two dozen terminals are currently located in Bobst library because it stays open late.

Like the dean of libraries, the director of academic computing is a member of the telecommunications committee.

Yet another area of service that involves the computer is the acquisition, cataloging, and servicing of machine-readable data files (MRDFs), such as census data tapes. In 1983-84, the library held several informational sessions with the computer center on availability and accessibility of MRDFs. Currently, the library receives many inquiries about the availability of computer tapes at NYU. Although the library is not in a position to store, load, or assist in the use of computer tapes, it nevertheless could play an important role in providing access to information about these files. To do so, it would be helpful if all MRDFs and their code books were deposited at the computer center. It also would be helpful to maintain lists and bibliographic records describing data files and code books available on campus for use by faculty and students. The library is eager to work with the computer center's staff in cataloging items stored in the center through the library's bibliographic utility, and to list them in BOBCAT with a computer-center location code. Once a new cataloging format for MRDFs is implemented, the library will be able to offer bibliographic assistance for this task. Both the University of Michigan and Princeton University have expressed interest in cataloging their collections by using this new format. As a result, cataloging copy would be available, thereby reducing the need for extensive original input of descriptive cataloging information.

The library's principal interest in MRDFs is to use its facilities and expertise to disseminate information about these files. Academic departments could assist in this access effort by depositing tapes with the computer center. In the dean's view, enhancing the cooperative relationship already established between the library and the computer center would foster the optimal use of information sources at NYU.

SUMMARY

Within less than a decade, the New York University libraries has made major advances in the use of new information technologies. During the tenure of the current dean of libraries, the library has implemented an online catalog, BOBCAT. The library also has been among the first units in the university to install a local area network.

These accomplishments become more significant when one considers the constraints under which the NYU library has operated. A decade ago, it was not an integrated entity, but rather a loosely connected group of 30 separate collections. The libraries, at what were then the two campuses of NYU, were completely separate administrative organizations. The limited financial resources of NYU as a whole posed another constraint. Financial difficulties that led to the divestiture of one campus in the 1970s have since been resolved, but not to a point at which the university is able to build up a comfortable margin of extra resources. Like all other units at NYU, the library has to compete for scarce institutional resources. Although fund raising has long been a university tradition, NYU is not considered to be a particularly well-endowed institution.

The current dean of libraries has eased some of these constraints and, in some cases, even turned them to advantages. Because of limited institutional resources, the deans at NYU are encouraged to pursue their own fund raising. By several accounts, the current dean of libraries has been successful in his entrepreneurial efforts to generate external support for the library, which in turn has facilitated implementation of automated systems in the library. He also has built cooperative relationships with other libraries through a consortial arrangement that he initiated. He has promoted cooperative efforts in information technology within NYU itself, for example, by proposing joint activities with the academic computing center in keeping track of machine-readable data files. Furthermore, as a member of the university's telecommunications committee, the current dean of libraries is actively involved in university plans for technological advances.

The library has benefited from the support of top university administrators, including the president and chancellor. This support, together with the current dean of libraries' strong belief in the benefits of new technologies, as reflected in the directions the library has taken during his tenure, can facilitate the attainment of his goal to transform the NYU library into "the integrator in an information environment."

UNIVERSITY OF GEORGIA

"It (the library) plays a crucial role in the strength of the University of Georgia's instructional and research programs. Without so distinguished and extensive a library collection, this institution could not have achieved the eminent position it now holds among large state universities throughout the United States."

The University of Georgia 1984: A Status Report

BACKGROUND

Institutional Profile

Since its founding in 1785, the University of Georgia has become a major teaching, research, and public service institution with more than 1,800 faculty members, 13 colleges, and a physical plant serving more than 25,000 students. The campus, including forestry and agricultural areas, covers nearly 43,000 acres. In addition, off-campus centers and experiment stations carry university services to all parts of the state.

Historically, teaching was the primary purpose of the University of Georgia and this continues to be a major responsibility. A special strength of the university lies in the scope and diversity of its degree programs. At the undergraduate level, the university offers 2 associate degrees and 15 baccalaureate degrees with concentrations in approximately 200 major fields through 117 academic departments. At the graduate level, 22 master's degrees are offered in 134 areas of concentration, as well as 40 specialist-in-education degrees and doctoral degrees (Ph.D., Ed.D., and D.P.A) in 84 areas. In addition, professional degree programs are available in accounting, forest resources, journalism, law, pharmacy, social work, and veterinary medicine.

The continuing vitality of the university's graduate educational programs depends not only on excellence in teaching, but also on a strong commitment to basic and applied research in all academic disciplines. In addition to training experts and scholars, the university seeks through research to expand the frontiers of knowledge by providing the expertise and resources necessary to cope with increasingly complex and difficult problems.

As a land-grant and sea-grant public institution, the University of Georgia has been a leader in the successful integration of teaching, research, and public service. In each of these mutually enhancing functions, the university has a stated commitment to excellence.

Library Profile

The University of Georgia libraries, with 2,316,499 volumes as of FY 1984, is the thirty-sixth largest academic library in the country. It is a highly centralized operation, consisting of three facilities: a social science and humanities library (the main library), a science library, and a law collection. The law library is separate organizationally from the other two, since it is administered by the law school (though included in the following statistics). The libraries have a professional staff of 74

FTE and a support staff of 163 FTE. Including student labor, total staff size is 324 FTE. Total expenditures for the library in FY 1984 were $7,355,431, of which $3,095,473 was spent on books, periodicals, and other research materials (*ARL Statistics, 1983-84*, Washington, D.C.: Association of Research Libraries, 1985).

The libraries provide information for the university's instructional, research, and public service activities. They conduct approximately 482,000 circulation transactions annually and service 25,000 interlibrary loan requests, including many from other institutions within the state. The libraries, open 97 hours per week during regular academic session, have seating for 1,300 in the main library, 1,000 in the science library, and 350 in the law library.

Materials collected by the libraries include manuscripts, broadsides, photographs, slides, filmstrips, motion pictures, sound recordings, audio and video tapes, music scores, and sheet music.

Source of Revenues and Level of Expenditures

Exhibits I and II indicate revenue sources and expenditure patterns for the University of Georgia in 1983-84. Expenditure patterns for the library are outlined in Exhibit III. State funds form the primary source of support for the library, although it also has a small endowment. The director of libraries restricts the use of these funds and of one-time gifts to expenditures for special collections. Income from such funds is estimated to be less than $100,000 per year. The director has established a policy concerning the maximum amount of interest from endowment that can be expended. Development efforts on behalf of the library have been integrated into the university's current capital campaign.

PLANNING AND MANAGEMENT PROCESSES

To obtain necessary information on planning and management processes, project staff met with key institutional administrators, including the president, vice president for academic affairs, vice president for business and finance, director of libraries, director of institutional research and planning, and assistant to the president for computing and information services. The findings in each of these areas are described below.

Organizational Structure

Organizational structures and reporting arrangements at the University of Georgia tend to be neither highly centralized nor highly regulated.

EXHIBIT I

The University of Georgia
Percent Distribution of Revenue by Source
FY 1974-75—1983-84

Source	74-75	75-76	76-77	77-78	78-79	79-80	80-81	81-82	82-83	83-84
State of Georgia	51.9%	49.8%	51.1%	51.4%	52.8%	53.1%	53.1%	55.0%	53.1%	55.0%
Counties of Georgia	1.6	1.7	1.6	1.7	1.7	1.8	1.7	1.6	1.7	1.9
Federal Appropriations	4.5	4.4	4.3	4.2	4.0	3.8	3.6	3.2	3.3	3.1
Student Tuition and Fees	9.9	11.3	10.8	9.7	8.7	8.3	9.2	9.4	10.1	10.1
Sales, Services, Miscellaneous	4.6	4.6	3.5	3.5	3.6	3.9	3.1	2.9	3.1	2.8
Gifts, Grants, Contracts	17.0	17.7	18.1	19.1	18.9	18.7	18.5	16.8	17.7	17.0
Auxiliary Enterprises	10.4	10.4	10.4	10.2	10.1	10.2	10.6	10.9	10.8	9.9
Endowment	0.1	0.1	0.2	0.2	0.2	0.2	0.2	0.2	0.2	0.2

Source: Office of the Vice President for Business and Finance

Percent Distribution of Revenue
By Source, FY 1983-84

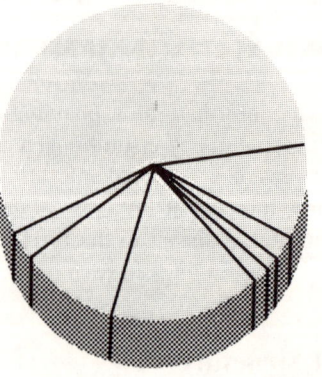

State of Georgia (55.0)

Student Tuition & Fees (10.1%)

Sales, Services, Miscellaneous (2.8%)

Federal Appropriations (3.1%)

Endowment (0.2%)

Georgia Counties (1.9%)

Auxiliary Enterprises (9.9%)

Gifts, Grants, Contracts (17.0%)

University of Georgia

EXHIBIT II

The University of Georgia
Percent Distribution of Expenditures by Budgetary Function
FY 1974-75—1983-84

Budgetary Function	74-75	75-76	76-77	77-78	78-79	79-80	80-81	81-82	82-83	83-84
Instruction	31.1%	30.5%	30.1%	32.3%	32.2%	31.2%	30.5%	30.1%	29.6%	29.6%
Research	17.1	18.3	18.4	19.1	19.1	19.9	19.4	19.4	19.4	19.5
Public Service	19.2	19.1	18.8	19.3	19.8	19.9	19.2	18.4	18.4	18.7
Academic Support	10.6	9.8	9.9	7.4	7.6	7.4	7.5	8.2	7.6	7.9
Student Services	1.5	1.5	1.6	1.4	1.3	1.5	1.5	1.5	1.5	1.7
Institutional Support	4.0	4.2	4.5	3.7	3.6	3.5	3.8	3.9	4.1	4.4
Physical Plant	6.4	6.4	6.7	7.0	6.7	6.6	7.9	8.1	8.2	7.8
Scholarships and Fellowships	1.2	.9	.7	.7	.7	.7	.7	.7	1.7	1.7
Auxiliary Enterprises	8.9	9.3	9.3	9.1	9.0	9.3	9.5	9.7	9.5	8.7

Source: Office of the Vice President for Business and Finance
(Based on HEGIS Reports)

Percent Distribution of Expenditures
By Budgetary Function, FY 1983-84

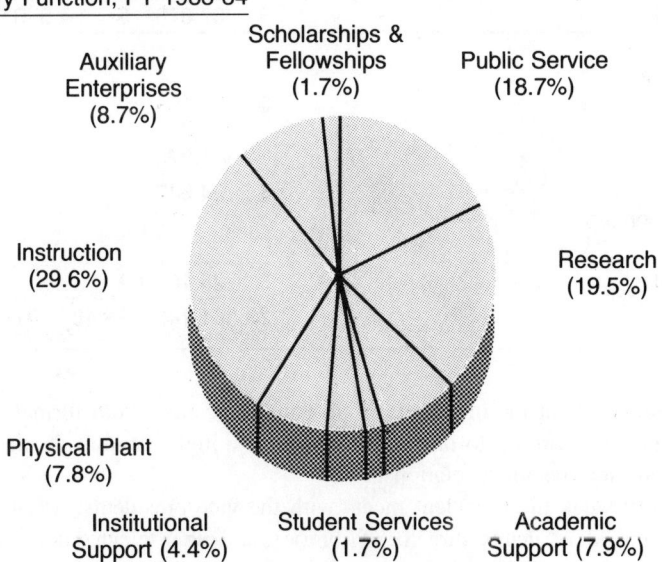

Auxiliary Enterprises (8.7%)
Scholarships & Fellowships (1.7%)
Public Service (18.7%)
Instruction (29.6%)
Research (19.5%)
Physical Plant (7.8%)
Institutional Support (4.4%)
Student Services (1.7%)
Academic Support (7.9%)

University Libraries in Transition

EXHIBIT III

University of Georgia Library Accounts
Fiscal Years 1981/82, 1982/83, and 1983/84

	1981/82	1982/83	1983/84
GENERAL OPERATIONS			
Personal Services			
Monthly	$1,552,136	$1,681,928	$1,785,907
Salaried	949,660	1,026,392	1,050,724
Hourly		2,463	
Students	300,957	308,507	262,854
	$2,802,753	$3,019,290	$3,099,485
Travel	34,357	33,976	33,105
Operating Expenses	98,026	97,577	98,971
Equipment	91,814	9,920	57,506
Total	$3,026,950	$3,160,763	$3,289,067
DATA PROCESSING			
Personal Services			
Monthly	$ 70,391	$ 80,228	$ 84,927
Operating Expenses	101,345	125,909	275,245
Equipment	69,414	67,915	29,518
Total	$ 241,150	$ 274,052	$ 389,690
SECURITY			
Personal Services	$ 61,116	$ 49,387	$ 47,303
Operating Expenses	6,762	5,589	5,252
Total	$ 67,878	$ 54,976	$ 52,555
PEABODY			
Personal Services			
Monthly	$ 15,154		
Salaried	8,523		
Students	1,270		
	$ 24,947		
Operating Expenses	217		
Equipment			
Total	$ 25,164	$	$
TOTAL	$3,361,142	$3,489,791	$3,731,312

The emphasis at the university is on communication, both formal and informal. According to one administrator, "a high premium is placed on good interpersonal relationships."

Every week the president meets with the vice presidents, assistants to the president, deans, director of libraries, and other selected university administrators. This meeting is followed by a meeting of executive officers only. Each month, the weekly meeting of senior administrators is expanded to include other officers, such as the director of institutional research and planning, the director of the computer center, and division heads within the College of Arts and Sciences. This group is known as the Academic Affairs Advisory Committee (AAAC).

The director of libraries, David Bishop, reports to the vice president for academic affairs. He is perceived as having dean's status but is on an annual contract. The director of libraries meets with his assistant directors once a week. There is also a weekly meeting with middle managers.

Planning

Planning at the institutional level tends to be integrated into the ongoing operations of the university. For example, the weekly deans' meeting and the AAAC serve as forums for reviewing institutional priorities and objectives. Rather than acting as formal planning sessions, these meetings serve to inform the president, vice presidents, and deans of ongoing developments at the institution. In September 1984, the university published a formal document titled *The University of Georgia 1984: A Status Report*. The document is intended to be a self-study and updated report on university progress toward achieving goals set in 1982. These goals are outlined in Exhibit IV.

Within the library, planning is the responsibility of the director and assistant directors. Again, planning is accomplished more by informal communication than as a stated function. There is, however, a formal plan for library automation, which sets forth six priority areas, including: (1) new capabilities, (2) enhancement of existing MARVEL capabilities, (3) data clean-up and maintenance, (4) data support systems, (5) architectural development and changes in MARVEL, and (6) planning and documentation. Details of the plan are presented later in this report.

The formal mechanism for obtaining faculty advice is the faculty library committee known as the "Library and Instructional Aids Committee." Informal contacts with faculty also keep the library director informed of faculty and institutional needs.

Budgeting

Since the University of Georgia is a public institution, its approach to budgeting is dictated largely by state processes and procedures. At the start of the budget process, individual units prepare their budgets and review them with their appropriate administrative officer. The library budget is submitted to the vice president for academic affairs. After an internal review process, the budget is submitted to the board of regents

EXHIBIT IV

Institutional Goals of the University of Georgia

Goal I
"To continue the University's progress toward becoming a world center in the fields of production, conversion, processing, marketing, and distribution, both nationally and internationally, of biomass."

Goal II
"To insure that hard-earned national prominence in certain areas, such as the natural and physical sciences, is not eroded. This in no way implies decreased support for other areas."

Goal III
"To remain an attractive opportunity for the best Georgia high school graduates and to maintain a suitable mix of students from out of state."

Goal IV
"To insure that every graduate of the University has attained an acceptable level of computer knowledge."

Goal V
"To institutionalize more completely the University's relationships with the private sector, both in the small business and corporate areas."

Goal VI
"To install and implement computing and other communications capabilities across the state so that all citizens can realize the benefits provided by the University in order that they may increase their productivity and knowledge. The delivery vehicle for this effort will be the service programs of the University."

Goal VII
"To continue to manage the University in the most cost-effective manner possible within the resources provided."

Goal VIII
"To continue to assess the economic climate and career opportunities in the state for the University's graduates and to modify the University's programs to meet those needs."

Goal IX
"To maintain at a high level the quest for outside, private funding, based on the recognition that the University will remain a 'state-assisted' institution and the measure of its quality will depend in part on outside private funding."

of the University of Georgia. The board has constitutional authority to govern, control, and manage the university system. These powers include authority for program approval or discontinuance, internal reallocation of the budget, facilities construction and decisions concerning the addition of new institutions, upgrading or downgrading the level of an institution, and closure or merger of institutions. The university system currently is composed of 33 institutions (4 university-level institutions, 14 senior colleges, and 15 junior colleges).

At budget hearings with the board of regents, the library is represented by the vice president for academic affairs. Funding for the university system is provided through a funding formula with five categories of need: (1) instruction and research, (2) public service, (3) academic support (which includes the library), (4) student services and instructional support, and (5) operation and maintenance of plant. Provisions also have been made for a quality-improvement fund that is intended to be an additional budget item not included in the formula and is designated as 1 percent of the total budget. It is important to note that the formula serves only as a basis for *requesting* funds from the legislature and is not used to *allocate* money to various institutions also. The appropriation to the university system is a lump sum and not an individual appropriation for each institution.

The library budget is segregated into three major categories of expenditure: library materials, personnel, and supplies and equipment. The library director has flexibility to move funds between expenditure categories. He also has control over lapsed salaries, or money available from unfilled positions in the library (salary savings). The director also has flexibility to transfer these funds to other expenditure categories. For example, salary savings can be used to offset insufficient funding in the student assistant budget and to pay for supplies and equipment. Such flexibility enables the director to respond to problem areas and to enhance the library operation. Salary savings, for example, have played a significant role in automating the library, since these funds have been used to purchase equipment.

The library is also the recipient of certain year-end, unexpended institutional funds. However, the director would prefer to have these funds at the start of a fiscal year, so that he could integrate them into his planning and budgeting process.

Implementation and Control

Controls on the library budget are largely imposed by the director. He will not, for example, transfer money out of the library materials budget without the advice and consent of the academic vice president. Since the materials budget, which is for user needs, is under severe economic pressure, this stricture is essential to indicate the library's high priority on meeting such needs. The emphasis on user needs is highlighted by the fact that despite an institutional midyear budget cut of $100,000, the book budget was increased by more than $300,000. This was accomplished because the library received some unexpected gifts and because of an aggressive use of endowment funds.

With regard to personnel management, a system of continuing appointment recently was developed by the library faculty and approved by the university administration. Continuing appointment, which is similar to tenure, provides job security for librarians who have demonstrated a high level of competence over an extended period. It also insures that those who fail to meet rigorous standards do not become part of permanent library faculty.

As noted, the process of implementing the budget is carried out under direction of vice presidents and deans. The president is kept informed through Monday morning deans' meetings, executive sessions with his senior administrators, and monthly AAAC meetings. It was noted during interviews that the president favors neither strong central control nor a plethora of policies that impede action or limit institutional responsiveness. In fact, the president, in addressing the issue of management, noted that "policies too frequently tend to make cowards of decision makers."

An accountant reports to the assistant director for administrative services for librarians. The accountant has been part of the university community for a number of years and has contacts throughout the institution. As a result, the library is able to function effectively within the financial and administrative structure of the institution. The management style of the director of libraries tends to mirror that of the president and his senior administrators. The director meets with his assistant directors as a group once a week. He also meets individually for one hour each week with each assistant director.

Evaluation

Evaluation at the institutional level is provided formally through a self-study process. Every ten years a self-study is completed for reaccreditation by the Southern Association of Colleges and Schools. In addition, regular accreditation self-studies are prepared by various colleges and programs for professional associations that accredit specific programs of study. Occasionally, special projects result in self-study, as in the case of the University System Needs Assessment Study requested by the university board of regents.

Informally, evaluation of institutional operations, including the library, is addressed during weekly meetings of the president with his deans and vice presidents, and through faculty and staff task forces and committees on specific operational areas, such as the library and instructional aids committee. Within the library various task forces, such as one on library automation, have been established. Informal contact between the director and individual faculty and staff members provides another mechanism for evaluating the effectiveness of library operations.

RESPONDING TO TECHNOLOGICAL CHANGE

For the University of Georgia, two factors heavily influenced development of automated library systems: (1) a strong commitment by the university to employ automated systems and (2) cooperation between the computer center and library staffs in developing and refining the library systems. To illustrate the influence of these factors, the library's approach to automation was reviewed in terms of: (1) configuration of the MARVEL system, (2) history of the system, (3) operational characteristics of the system, (4) refinements to the system, and (5) future efforts in library automation.

Configuration of the MARVEL System

The university library's core system, known as MARVEL, involves a book acquisitions system (including ordering, receipt, and payment), a circulation system, and an experimental, online public access catalog (OPAC). Eighty terminals are attached to the library system, seven of which are for public use.

The library catalogs books through the nationally based Online Computer Library Center (OCLC). The OCLC system also is used for interlibrary lending and borrowing. There are ten OCLC terminals in the library.

The library also houses a cluster of 14 PLATO terminals, which are used heavily by the faculties of the music and Latin departments.

Operation of the MARVEL system is overseen by the director of the libraries, who has experience as a programmer and systems analyst, and by his assistant directors. The computer center hires and trains personnel to operate the system and the library pays their salaries. Currently, there are seven programmer positions dedicated to the library system. In addition to the latter, there are two other major systems on campus: one for administrative and one for academic functions.

In order to place development of the MARVEL system in the context of the institution's overall computer strategy, it should be noted that goal six of the overall institutional plan is:

> "To install and implement computing and other communications capabilities across the state so that all citizens can realize the benefits provided by the university in order that they may increase their productivity and knowledge. The delivery vehicle for this effort will be the service programs of the university."

In furtherance of this goal, the campus of the University of Georgia had 16 computer service centers in 1983, with a total of 349 access ports. By the fall of 1984, four more computer service centers were in operation, adding 90 terminals to the total access ports. These computer service centers contain a variety of computer facilities, including mainframe, mini- and microcomputer terminals, along with a regular staff for planning and consulting with users.

The University of Georgia also has received combined state and private funding for establishing an Advanced Computational Methods Center (ACMC), an agency that is to focus on research and development of a new generation of "supercomputers." This center is planned to be the site for work on complex problems in such diverse fields as aerospace, agriculture, construction, and chemical engineering. With implementation of plans for the ACMC, the University of Georgia will become a national leader in research and development of fifth-generation computers.

Other innovations in facilities and software at the university include replacement of the present oncampus telecommunications system; provision of a bypass carrier system for data communications on the campus; and upgrading of MARVEL software for the university library, which will result in a completely integrated library automation system.

Along with the strong emphasis on acquisition of fifth-generation machines and other improvements in facilities, there is equal university emphasis on outreach programs dedicated to enhancing a better understanding of the applicability and utility of computer technology.

History of the MARVEL System

A key factor in development and refinement of the MARVEL system has been the cooperation and support of the computer center. The system was conceived by the former director of libraries, and an assistant director for systems and services. During development, there was some resistance from within the library to the system. This resistance stemmed from the perception that the director of libraries had not involved other library personnel in developing the system and that the library staff as a whole had not had an opportunity to "buy" into either the system or the concepts that led to its development.

When the current director of libraries was hired, he expressed some concern over the utility of the system, which he felt could not serve as an effective online, public access catalog (OPAC) in its present configuration. He suggested using the system for data processing and inputting the data into a purchased OPAC. However, computer center staff felt that the system could be salvaged and within six months they had made necessary improvements. This commitment by the computer center to the MARVEL system and the center's good relationship with the library are two principal reasons why MARVEL has been so effective for the University of Georgia.

In retrospect, it appears that the major reasons why the director of libraries decided to stay with the MARVEL system were:

1. The system provided a relational data base, in that parts of a record are stored in separate files, and are assembled when the user presents a query. This produces a slower response time, but better file organization.
2. There was an historical commitment to the system by the university, computer center, and the library.
3. The basic structure of the system was sound.
4. The system provided the library with a certain degree of autonomy in that the library was not dependent on external vendors for system repairs or modifications.

Concerning any future system revisions, the director of libraries indicated that an attempt is being made to develop a management-by-exception approach through automatic maintenance of online systems. Under this approach, most activities would be reduced to batch-processing modes, with interactive processes used only for exceptions. The current plan is to accept standard records and run them through batch programs to insure that they are consistent with the library's data base, to which they would then be added. Only those records that either are not consistent with the database or that have computer-identifiable errors are to be examined. In this regard, the library would rebuild the batch-data processing capability that went out of fashion with the advent of online systems.

Operational Characteristics of the System

One of the most interesting statistics concerning operation of the library system is that the level of cataloging activity at the university has increased by 98 percent in four years. The reason for this increase relates both to changes in operating procedures and use of the MARVEL system.

When the director of libraries assumed his present position, he found that there were few cataloging standards. As a consequence, he established standards and then modified them after a time in accordance with the volume and operational characteristics of the cataloging department.

In using the MARVEL system, a process was introduced whereby the library attempted to minimize the level of original cataloging. The process operates as follows: If a catalog record is not found in OCLC, the book is placed in a public in-process collection, which is accessible through using temporary records in the MARVEL online catalog. Periodically, records in MARVEL for this collection are searched, in batch mode, against cataloging tapes from the Library of Congress, purchased by the library for this purpose. If a "hit" is made, the book is cataloged. If not, the book remains on the shelf for original cataloging or for another search at a later time.

Another aspect of library automation that has prompted a good deal of discussion, both within and outside the university community, is the use and level of user fees. At the University of Georgia, a fee has been established for online searching under which a user pays the actual amount of search up to a specified ceiling. If the cost is greater than the ceiling, the user pays the ceiling figure and the library pays the additional cost. The ceiling amount varies among data bases, depending on the cost of searching each one. For example, maximum charges for ERIC and for Chemical Abstracts are $3.75 and $10.20, respectively. The maximum charge is generally computed at 15 percent of the hourly charge. This fee is adjusted to the user's advantage when the same database is offered through different systems.

The online search fee structure is intended to serve as a regulating mechanism and not as a basis for cost recovery. When this service was first introduced there was a surge in usage, which subsequently declined. In discussing this phenomenon with faculty, the director concluded that heavy use of bibliographic databases occurs only at limited times during research—at start-up, when searching the relevant literature, and near conclusion, when verifying references. In contrast, during active research there is a need only to check recent additions to database files, which involves merely a limited search.

In interlibrary loans, the university library charges users for photocopies and other direct costs of service, but it does not recover support costs.

Refinements to the System

Major hardware improvements to the MARVEL system occurred during 1983-84. The CDC OMEGA computer was replaced by an IBM 370/158, which resulted in an increase in computing capability of approximately 100 percent. At midyear the IBM Series One, which collects circulation transactions, was replaced by a larger version of the same machine. This upgrade, in addition to improving performance, allowed the library to move more circulation functions from the main computer to the Series One. The final hardware improvement was the addition of eight 30350 dual-density disk units. These units increased the library's mass storage capacity by 120 percent, and will allow it to expand its data files for years to come.

A major automated systems development during 1983-84 was the implementation of an online, public-access catalog. A task force of library and systems staff spent more than a year learning what had been done or was being planned in various other libraries. Using results of that study, the group developed specifications for an online catalog that is potentially a leader among systems of its type in the country.

Future Activities in Library Automation

In August 1984, the library held an automation planning session, of which the principal outcome was development of an agenda for future automation activities related to the library. This agenda is outlined in Exhibit V, where several items are worthy of further discussion. First, one criticism leveled against the MARVEL system was that it was weak on management-decision support systems and management data systems. To address this concern, a program to provide management data on library operations is to be developed. Specific components of this program are to include:
1. A system for transaction logs
2. A circulation statistics package
3. A procedure to produce tailored samples for the MARVEL to MARC IV format for testing and evaluation
4. A procedure for technically processing management reports

A second area of refinement involves a program that would provide dial-up and remote access to MARVEL from sites both on and off campus and would make MARVEL available through terminals and departments throughout the university. The planned implementation by the university of a local area network (LAN) should help to further this process.

EXHIBIT V

Agenda for Automation of the University of Georgia Library

I. *New Capabilities*
   A. Incorporation of the serials-holding format into MARVEL
   B. Use of OCLC records in MARVEL for ordering
   C. Electronic Mail System
   D. Development of management information for MARVEL (e.g., government documents (GPO tapes); Center for Research Libraries data, etc.)
   E. Integration of external databases into MARVEL
   F. Provision of remote access to MARVEL
   G. Automation of reserves
   H. Serial control system

II. *Enhancement of Existing MARVEL Capabilities*
   A. Improvement of menu flows, commands, searching options in the processing system of MARVEL
   B. Processing system enhancements
   C. Improvement of menu flows, commands, searching options in the Online Catalog
   D. Bibliographic reports

III. *Data Clean-up and Maintenance*
   A. Bibliographic database maintenance
   B. Clean-up of bibliographic database
   C. Retrospective conversion
   D. Processing database maintenance
   E. Clean-up of processing database

IV. *Data Support System*
   A. Archival records from OCLC
   B. Use and maintenance of LC MARC records
   C. Blackwell/North America development program
   D. LC authority maintenance program

V. *Architectural Development and Changes in MARVEL*
   A. Development of MARVEL to MARC format
   B. Development and implementation of new data structure in MARVEL
   C. Addition of discrete databases to the Online Catalog, e.g., AGRICOLA, ERIC, etc.
   D. Development of capacity for nonpublic records or data
   E. Index design
   F. MARVEL record structure made MARC-compatible

EXHIBIT V (continued)

Agenda for Automation of the University of Georgia Library

VI. *Planning and Documentation*
  A. Establishment of a staffing structure for librarywide involvement in developing and maintaining MARVEL
  B. Documentation and training for MARVEL

In a third area, the library will explore the feasibility of providing bibliographic output from the system in various forms to meet the specifications or "profile" defined by the user (patron or staff). For users of the online catalog, this program would include the capability to request a print-out of desired records. In a related area, a program is to be designed to add discrete databases to the online catalog, for example, AGRICOLA, ERIC, etc. As separate files that can be accessed and searched in MARVEL, these discrete databases already include their own access systems. Among other features, this program would provide the capability to search for citations to periodical literature in selected subject areas.

Finally, the plan calls for documentation and training for MARVEL. A program to write documentation is to be prepared that will describe the system and facilitate its use. It is planned that training will become an ongoing program to enable staff to keep current with system changes. Training will be a regular feature for new staff.

SUMMARY

It is clear from discussions with both institutional and library administrators that they recognize the library's importance to the continued growth and development of the university. Commitment to the library is shown not only by financial support, but also by the inclusion of the director of libraries in major decision-making bodies of the university and the high degree of flexibility he is permitted in operating the library. In part, this support and recognition have been fostered by the management style of the director of libraries, who places great value on keeping others informed of library operations and, more important, on staying attuned to institutional priorities and library-user needs. In this regard, the library attempts to initiate programs and services to meet user needs rather than to react solely to user demands.

The movement toward automation at the University of Georgia has benefited from two factors. First, there is a commitment on the part of the university to be in the forefront both in terms of computer systems and computer literacy. Such a commitment fosters an attitude of innovation, which is translated into a desire to explore how institutional activities may benefit from advances in computer technology. The MARVEL system grew out of this environment.

A second major factor in the evolution of automated systems was the commitment of the computer center to work with the library in developing and maintaining the MARVEL system. In part, this attitude was nurtured by the approach of the director of libraries toward the computer center. During an interview, he indicated that "one of the biggest problems of library directors relative to automation is that they try to do the computer center's job. They try to make decisions that the computer center should make." Rather than assuming this posture, the director of libraries has worked together with the computer center staff to develop and refine the MARVEL system.

In summary, David Bishop, the current director of libraries, believes that the future of university libraries will be determined by their ability to move beyond traditional methods of providing library services and toward the innovative use of technology to better meet the needs of library users. In this regard the University of Georgia libraries are in tune with the priorities and objectives of the university as a whole.

NACUBO Board of Directors

Pete Reid, President, *Whitman College*
John A. Falcone, Vice President/President-elect, *Lafayette College*
John D. Mulholland, Secretary, *Indiana University*
George J. Ruschell, Treasurer, *University of Kentucky*
Paul J. Aslanian, *Macalester College*
Joe H. Barber, Jr., *Mississippi College*
Charlotte V. Berry, *California State University*
George Davis, Jr., *Montgomery College*
Lyman J. Durfee, *Brigham Young University*
William L. Erickson, *San Diego State University*
Joe F. Evans, *Washington University*
Peter G. Geil, *Wittenberg University*
Robert L. Goudie, *Atlantic Community College*
Margaret M. Healy, *Bryn Mawr College*
James E. Morley, Jr., *Cornell University*
R. Eugene Smith, *Memphis State University*
Paula I. Thomas, *University of Southern California*
Jerry R. Tubbs, *Central Michigan University*
Lucius A. Williams, *Tuskegee University*

James A. Hyatt, Interim Executive Vice President

**NATIONAL ASSOCIATION OF
COLLEGE AND UNIVERSITY BUSINESS OFFICERS
ONE DUPONT CIRCLE, SUITE 500
WASHINGTON, DC 20036
(202) 861-2500**